The Confidence Book

Gordon Lamont is a radio producer, writer, actor and trainer. Through his company, Creative Training, he's worked with the BBC, Channel 4, Actors Centre in Business, DfES, DTI and smaller companies and organizations, including schools. Many of his courses and much of his coaching involve work on confidence, and it was this that gave him the idea for *The Confidence Book*.

His previous books include *Work–Life Balance*, with Ronni Lamont (Sheldon Press, 2001), *The Creative Path* (Azure, 2004) and *The Creative Teacher*, with Rosemary Hill (Arts Council, 2005). The author has created a website to accompany this book; it provides more confidence tips and the opportunity for readers to post their own ideas. You can find The Confidence Site at <www.theconfidencesite.co.uk>.

Overcoming Common Problems Series

Selected titles

A full list of titles is available from Sheldon Press,
36 Causton Street, London SW1P 4ST and on our website at
www.sheldonpress.co.uk

Assertiveness: Step by Step
Dr Windy Dryden and Daniel Constantinou

Breaking Free
Carolyn Ainscough and Kay Toon

Calm Down
Paul Hauck

Cataract: What You Need to Know
Mark Watts

Cider Vinegar
Margaret Hills

Comfort for Depression
Janet Horwood

Confidence Works
Gladeana McMahon

Coping Successfully with Pain
Neville Shone

Coping Successfully with Panic Attacks
Shirley Trickett

Coping Successfully with Period Problems
Mary-Claire Mason

Coping Successfully with Prostate Cancer
Dr Tom Smith

Coping Successfully with Ulcerative Colitis
Peter Cartwright

Coping Successfully with Your Hiatus Hernia
Dr Tom Smith

Coping Successfully with Your Irritable Bowel
Rosemary Nicol

Coping with Alopecia
Dr Nigel Hunt and Dr Sue McHale

Coping with Age-related Memory Loss
Dr Tom Smith

Coping with Blushing
Dr Robert Edelmann

Coping with Bowel Cancer
Dr Tom Smith

Coping with Brain Injury
Maggie Rich

Coping with Candida
Shirley Trickett

Coping with Chemotherapy
Dr Terry Priestman

Coping with Childhood Allergies
Jill Eckersley

Coping with Childhood Asthma
Jill Eckersley

Coping with Chronic Fatigue
Trudie Chalder

Coping with Coeliac Disease
Karen Brody

Coping with Cystitis
Caroline Clayton

Coping with Depression and Elation
Patrick McKeon

Coping with Down's Syndrome
Fiona Marshall

Coping with Dyspraxia
Jill Eckersley

Coping with Eating Disorders and Body Image
Christine Craggs-Hinton

Coping with Eczema
Dr Robert Youngson

Coping with Endometriosis
Jo Mears

Coping with Epilepsy
Fiona Marshall and Dr Pamela Crawford

Coping with Gout
Christine Craggs-Hinton

Coping with Hearing Loss
Christine Craggs-Hinton

Coping with Heartburn and Reflux
Dr Tom Smith

Coping with Incontinence
Dr Joan Gomez

Coping with Macular Degeneration
Dr Patricia Gilbert

Overcoming Common Problems Series

Overcoming Common Problems Series

Overcoming Common Problems

The Confidence Book

GORDON LAMONT

First published in Great Britain in 2007

Sheldon Press
36 Causton Street
London SW1P 4ST

The author and publisher have made every effort to ensure that the
external website and email addresses included in this book are correct and
up to date at the time of going to press. The author and publisher are not
responsible for the content, quality or continuing accessibility of the sites.

British Library Cataloguing-in-Publication Data
A catalogue record for this book is available from the British Library

ISBN 978-1-84709-001-0

1 3 5 7 9 10 8 6 4 2

Typeset by Fakenham Photosetting Ltd, Fakenham, Norfolk
Printed in Great Britain by Ashford Colour Press

Contents

Acknowledgements

I'd like to thank the following training and development colleagues whose expertise has given me confidence:

Mary Hartley for her generous help with the body language material and for our regular and much valued freelance and writing chats.

At Ian Peacock's Talk Consultancy <www.talkconsultancy.com>, I'd like to thank Kathleen Griffin, Henrietta Bond and, of course, Ian himself for his dynamic leadership and creativity.

At Talkshow Communication <www.talkshowcommunication.com>: Jonathan Halls, whose innovative yet down-to-earth approach makes him a sought-after training provider and inspirational speaker.

At Actors Centre in Business <www.actorscentreinbusiness.co.uk>: Tracy Thomson, who's like a breath of the freshest air in the jargon-filled world of training; also Michael John and all colleagues at the Actors Centre – a great place to work.

At BBC Training <www.bbctraining.com>: Matt Foster, Fran Acheson and Ros Toynbee (as I write, taking up a new training and development leadership role at GE Money); my fellow freelancer Simon Major <www.soundscreative.org>, from whom I've learnt tons as we've run our Trainer Training courses together.

Fiona Marshall at Sheldon Press has been the best editor and one whom I've never needed a confidence-boost to approach.

Finally my wife Ronni, not only for making helpful suggestions and offering ideas but for all the other stuff...

Gordon Lamont
www.creativetraining.org.uk
www.theconfidencesite.co.uk

Introduction

Confidence is not about feelings as we so often think. Confidence is about doing. This book is about finding ways to do and letting the feelings follow on. You'll find many books that promise 'a new you' by doing this or that, sticking rigidly to one plan or another. All of these books (and DVDs and websites) have their followers and all will have people who have been helped, even had their lives transformed, so I'm not writing in order to knock anyone else's approach. I know and respect neuro-linguistic programming (NLP) teachers and practitioners, dreamwork experts, behavioural therapists, hypnotherapists and many people who can legitimately claim to offer techniques, support and success in helping people to overcome difficulties, including a lack of confidence. At heart, however, I simply don't believe that we know enough about how our thoughts, emotions and consciousness combine to create a sense of self to be able to offer one-approach-fits-all techniques to being more confident. So I am not claiming that this book will change your life. Too many self-help gurus offer a false vision of a perfect future. It's comforting but unrealistic. For me, and therefore for this book, there is no point in trying to give a system, an answer that will change everything for ever. Although there are systematic approaches and answers aplenty in the book, they are all based on the notion that you and I are different, that our thinking patterns will have some things in common and some divergence; that what seems obvious to me may be questionable to you, and that what you find helpful I may find obstructing. We also change with time, so the things that work well for you today may be inappropriate in a month's or a year's time. This is another factor that the one-size-fits-all systems tend to ignore.

So this book takes a different approach. We will not try to become more confident people, to change the way we are, the way we feel; rather we'll go at it from the other end and focus on achievement. So the question is not, 'How can I feel more confident in order to make that phone call I've been dreading'; it is 'How can I prepare to make that phone call to give myself the best chance of success?' If you attack things this way round you'll find that the feelings get dragged along by the action. It's like so many things: focus on the feelings and they become dominant; take action and the feelings can no longer rule.

> Will not a tiny speck very close to our vision blot out the glory
> of the world, and leave only a margin by which we see the blot?
> I know no speck so troublesome as self.
>
> (George Eliot, *Middlemarch*)

How to use this book

The book is in three main chapters. Chapter 1, 'Getting started', gives some initial exercises to get you started on your own confidence work by thinking about your thoughts, feelings and actions in relation to confidence and focusing on those things you want to work on. Chapter 2, 'Confidence toolkit', takes major areas that have arisen from workshops, coaching and discussions, and attempts to explore them in some detail, offering practical exercises, advice and tips. Chapter 3 was originally titled 'Fifty confidence boosters', but it's grown a bit! These are quick-reference ideas, things you can dip in and out of; they are designed to give you something to try out in a brief, snappy format. In some cases the techniques, approaches and tips are amplified elsewhere in the book.

It's probably best to read through and, as far as you find it helpful, work through the first two chapters – 'Getting started' and the 'Confidence toolkit'; you can then dip in and out of Chapter 3, 'Sixty-three confidence boosters' – and there's a prize for anyone who tries them all: the satisfaction of knowing that you're probably a very rounded, tolerant, relaxed and unique individual!

There are bound to be things in here that are not for you, approaches that are too obvious, too left-field or simply inappropriate for your situation, but I believe that confidence is closely linked to creativity, that '1 + 1 = New' (is it getting too left-field already?), and that what we often need is the impetus to break out of the way we've always thought, the way we've allowed ourselves to picture our character and our lives; so my plea is: don't reject something as too radical until you've given it a go as it might just be the confidence key you need for a particular situation.

Why did I write this book?

The money? I won't deny there's some, but neither have you contributed to my still imaginary luxury villa (especially if you haven't bought this yet).

The kudos? Perhaps I won't be on TV promoting this bestseller, but then again, perhaps I will (gotta show some confidence here!); either way, I'm sure I'll slip 'My new book' into many a training and coaching session.

Because someone said 'Yes'? Of course – what a confidence boost if someone's prepared to commission.

The question I'm really asking is: 'Why me?' Am I a particularly confident person with pearls of wisdom to dispense from my lofty heights of success? No, but I do have a working life that used to be called, with the height of late–1990s trendiness, 'portmanteau living'; this is the idea that instead of having a job, I do a number of things and combine them in varying degrees at different times to make a working life. So, currently for me the portmanteau includes: writing and producing/directing radio programmes; book editorial; education website commissioning;

editorial, media and management training; acting; book writing; creativity consultancy; and a bit more. I'm aware that this could sound like showing off, or at the other end of the scale like being an odd-job man, but these are simply the bits – and sometimes they are very bitty bits – that I put together to make a living. It works most of the time, although I still face the 'feast or famine' principle: weeks of too much to do and opportunities missed because of busyness, followed by a month or more of knocking on doors and feeling that we're all off to the poorhouse. That's the freelance life, and you have to live with it. I enjoy the variety, it fits my easily bored personality, but it does call for confidence or, in keeping with the theme of this book, the ability to get things done despite sometimes feeling unconfident. There are examples of when I've felt less than confident scattered throughout the book, so I hope it's clear that I'm not 'ConfidentMan' riding to the rescue; just an average human, who's got to cope.

The other reason for writing the book is that some of my work in management training, role-play and personal development touches on these issues, so I've been able to draw on those experiences for some of the examples, suggestions and case studies in the book.

1

Getting started

One day at the shops

I was about seven and I'd saved up my pocket money to buy a model boat that I'd seen in a shop. We went to town. The boat wasn't there. I didn't know what to do. I'd had my heart set on it, though goodness knows why as I've never had any interest in boats whatsoever; but there it was – gone. I bought a set of skittles instead and then felt terrible all the way home. Had I wasted my money? I wished I still had my shilling or whatever it was; maybe the boat would be back next week but I wouldn't be able to buy it. I felt deep confusion, upset and sadness as probably only a child can. Emotions can completely overwhelm us before we have developed the rational skills to at least have a hope of dealing and working with them. Interestingly, I still have a similar though less intense feeling when making big decisions about money; it's probably an area that I'd say I'm not very confident in, and this makes me quite conservative – or mean, as my family might say.

Exercise 1.1

Think about your own childhood through the lens of confidence. Pick on one incident or story as I did. Perhaps one in which you acted confidently or unconfidently, or one in which you felt self-assured or threatened and fearful.

   As a way of starting to think about your own confidence story, recall this incident in as much detail as possible and with a focus on feelings, and ask yourself the questions below. They can be quite demanding so give yourself plenty of thinking time, perhaps a few minutes at a time over several days and, if you find this at all upsetting, don't be too hard on yourself.

5

- What does this story tell me about my confidence at the time?
- What words can I use to accurately describe the feelings accompanying the story?
- Do any of these feelings related to my confidence still apply in adult life?
- How would I compare my confidence then and now?

Exercise 1.2

This exercise is adapted (actually, pretty much copied verbatim) from my fellow Talk Consultancy confidence trainer, Kathleen Griffin. Kathleen is the author of *The Forgiveness Formula: Why Letting Go Is Good for You and How to Make It Happen* (Simon & Schuster, 2003), which I think is fairly descriptive as titles go. Kathleen's workshops quickly and clearly help people to understand their confidence issues and see them in a new light. The exercise is based on family trees.

1 Take a piece of paper – large is good but A4 will do – and think about your relations: your parents, grandparents, brothers and sisters, aunts and uncles and so on. Draw a simple family tree, but don't worry too much about leaving gaps or getting the details right. The important thing is to end up with something that you can work on, so completeness isn't the name of the game.

2 Look at your family tree as if through a confidence lens. What do you see? Which of these relationships had the biggest effect on your confidence as you grew up? Which enhanced your confidence and which undermined or stifled it? Have any of these relationships created confidence issues that have lasted into adulthood?

3 Repeat the exercise by thinking about your friends and your current network of relationships: who makes you feel confident now, and who destabilizes you?

It's early days in your confidence work, but you might like to begin to think about how you can make the most of those confidence-boosting relationships and the extent to which you value the others and whether they can be 'turned' to become more positive.

Don't worry if this seems like a tall order; put your charts to one side and continue with the exercises in this book. Then come back to your charts when you've done some more confidence thinking and planning. As you work through this book, you should find that you have plenty of new strategies with which to approach your relationships in a more confident fashion.

Confidence in odd situations – three days in Cambridge

Let's fast-forward 40-odd years from that day when the boat wasn't in, to show how confidence can fluctuate in strange or new situations.

One of my regular jobs is to teach radio drama skills and improvisation to actors at the Actors Centre in London and occasionally at the Northern Actors Centre in Manchester. As a member of the Actors Centre I can take advantage of the great range of classes on offer and I've discovered that I love improvisation. After a couple of years of working there and getting to know people, I was asked by a fellow tutor to join a small company that was putting together a one-off devised performance. I was delighted, and joined the small company in Cambridge for a week of devising a piece very loosely based on Strindberg's *Miss Julie*. By the morning of the first day I was starting to feel a little awkward. It soon became clear that there wasn't a real role for me. The director had the idea that I should 'counterpoint the action' by appearing as if I were the director of the piece lurking around the outside of the performance, never speaking but leaning in and out and in fact just 'being there'.

Strange things began to happen. Our lead was someone with a profile on the comedy circuit and prime-time TV appearances under her belt who wanted to try some avant-garde theatre. She suddenly got a job abroad and pretty much as soon as she'd said 'Hello', off she went, missing the whole devising process with a promise to be back on the day of the performance. The creative solution to this was to double with two other actors playing

Julie, sometimes alternately and sometimes consecutively. One spoke in her native Norwegian, the other in a voice that she based on Minnie Mouse. I was in a strange place. I have great respect for the actors and the director but in this case their place wasn't mine. I was lost, lurking in the shadows, feeling odd, unnecessary and out of place.

My confidence plummeted. At one point I opted out of a discussion because I didn't know how I fitted in, or how to contribute constructively. I remember feeling that soon I would not be fully in control of my actions. I think it was fight-or-flight taking over, and the latter won the day. After three days I made my excuses to the director (who I think was glad to get rid of me), and slipped away.

At the end of the week, my wife and I, in a confident gesture, went to see the one-off production. We discovered that my role had been replaced by someone who did indeed wander around the production, but as a creative touch he had a pair of speakers around his neck playing house and techno so that as he moved closer to people, presumably to bring the focus towards them, he drowned out anything they might be saying – though Minnie cut through admirably! The comedian lead coped with dignity after her absence abroad for pretty much the whole devising process, but I suspect that she was delighted that no press were present and that she'd made a bit of money on EuroTV that week. It was a bit like a trip back to the 1970s, when this kind of production was first 'hip', as we used to say then, right down to the request, once the show petered out, for the audience to join the cast on stage to dance. No one did, although I would have done if I could have got out of my against-the-wall seat – honest. After a shuffling silence, a voice called out, 'What the **** was that all about?' One very sharp actor instantly replied,

'It's all about the champagne that's waiting in the bar. Let's go.'

I reckoned that I'd had a lucky escape. Or maybe, on reflection, it was my confident behaviour that gave me the gumption to walk out when I found it wasn't for me. I must say, though, that I certainly didn't feel confident at the time.

There is no such being as a confident person. Everyone has situations in which his or her confidence is undermined by a certain set of circumstances, or an unexpected situation in which he or she does not feel secure. Here's a case in point from a very experienced media professional who found herself working in a new way:

> I've been producing *Xxxx* for a fortnight, and that has been interesting from the confidence point of view. I started with new technology and little training, and had to do an interview down the line with the presenter. I wished to appear as if I knew what I was doing, even though I didn't really know how to work the mixing desk. I found someone to help and it was all fine. But then I had to go back and edit at my desk and found the technology just didn't work, which involved getting others to come and sort it out. All fine in the end, but I was so stressed – partly from having to show confidence to the presenter – that I found I couldn't eat my lunch! This has never happened to me before. Today we had to mix the programme and it was all fine...

Exercise 1.3: What situations sap your confidence?

1 Spend a few moments reflecting on specific instances when you have felt a lack of confidence. Have you ever felt anything akin to the fight-or-flight situation I describe above? Has a feeling of a lack of confidence come upon you unexpectedly and taken you by surprise?
2 Can you see any common threads emerging in these situations; does this lead you to identify the things that trigger these feelings and behaviour?
3 Fill in the table on the next page – there are some examples first.

I feel confident when ...	I feel unconfident when ...
I'm in my routine and everything's where it should be.	I don't know what I'm supposed to do.
I understand what my role is.	I'm not sure what people expect of me.
I'm with my family.	I'm with my family.

Exercise 1.4

1 Take a sheet of paper and draw a confident-looking stick-figure in the middle.
2 Write all around the figure any words or short phrases that come to mind when you think about confidence. It's important not to self-censor – this is when we have a thought and then stop it, perhaps because we think it's too obvious or too obscure, too embarrassing or simply 'wrong'. This exercise is for your eyes only, so you can be open and honest and simply let what occurs to you form part of the exercise – no need to censor. So if confidence makes you think of toothpaste (because of the 'Colgate ring of confidence', if you can remember back that far), simply go with it. This is valuable because of the way that one thought leads to another; for example, thinking about toothpaste might lead you to thinking about appearance or hygiene worries or being manipulated by adverts. If you closed down the toothpaste thought, you might not get to the others queuing along behind it.

3   Take a look at the words and circle the three that seem most important to you. Which three words or short phrases speak most potently to you? Take three new sheets of paper and write one of these at the top of each.

4   Write or draw a short account based on your own experience and relating to that word. So for example:

You may be wondering why I've suggested drawing a confident stick-figure and the possibility of drawing your responses. It's simply that some readers will feel more comfortable with visual rather than written material, and for all of us, whether we consider ourselves able to sketch or not, it's good to use different parts of the brain to enliven us and get the creative thinking juices flowing. You'll be able to adapt many of the suggestions in this book to your own preferred style of working, so feel free to replace words with pictures and to do your thinking on paper, out loud or in your head, as suits you.

Exercise 1.5

Can you pull together the exercises so far to complete a confidence audit statement like the case study example below? Use the headings to give your statement structure.

As a child...
I gained my sense of confidence from academic success but my confidence was undermined by bullying and the fact that I thought there was no one I could talk to about it.

As an adult...
I am only confident with a very small group of friends and family and even then I am easily undermined by what I perceive to be unkind words. I read too much into things and always think that others are thinking the worst of me.

My confidence comes from...
When I stop and look back at what I've achieved. I know that I'm well respected at work and although family life is never easy, I'm proud of my children and my husband.

My lack of confidence comes from ...
Inner voices telling me that I am not an attractive person and that other people are brighter than me.

My focus will be...
Working through this book I want to focus on understanding and then dealing with those inner voices: where do they come from, why are they so powerful and how can I stop them sapping my confidence?

Finally

You'll find a range of confidence-boosting techniques and tips in the pages of this book. None of them is rocket science, most are simply common sense; some are counter-intuitive, some may be too arty-farty for your taste and some will seem too obvious or too detached from your situation. Take what's useful but do challenge yourself to try new things and not immediately to say 'That's not for me'.

As I said at the start of the Introduction, confidence is not about feelings as we so often think; confidence is about doing. This book is about finding ways to do and letting the feelings follow on.

2

Confidence toolkit

In this chapter I'm going to focus on some practical ideas for achieving your goals with greater confidence. It's not about changing who you are into someone you're not; it's all about identifying particular things you want to achieve but feel a lack of confidence about. The various ideas, exercises and techniques in this chapter will help you get there and will enable you to overcome feelings of inadequacy and self-doubt. That last sentence is so important in my whole approach to confidence: it's about overcoming, about achievement. Let me set that in context with an example: supposing that you want to send in to a magazine a short story, article or perhaps a letter, but feel that your work is not good enough and that you'll not get it published. Which is better: to attempt to become a different person with the magic ingredient Factor C(onfidence), or to learn to look objectively at the situation and find strategies to achieve your goal of sending in the work. I think it's the second option, and that's what the ideas here are all about – the confidence to achieve; do that and the feelings will sort themselves out.

The ideas in this chapter fall into the following categories, each of which is given its own section.

1 Relaxation
2 Body language
3 Appearance
4 Feelings, thoughts and core beliefs
5 Visualization, memory and imagination
6 Learning your stuff!

7 Small talk

8 Creativity and confidence: the Quintessence method

I suggest reading the whole chapter and then trying out what seems most appropriate for you and for your situation – and, of course, feel free to adapt, combine and develop.

1 Relaxation

I've put this at the top of this chapter because so many of the approaches that follow benefit from gaining some perspective and seeing things more objectively. Simple relaxation techniques can play a large part in putting us in the right frame of mind for this.

Location

You can use relaxation techniques anywhere; you might be commuting by train or bus; you might be walking or you might be at home or at work or in a specially created quiet space – at home or in a church, for example, or even in a shopping centre, some of which now have a 'quiet space'. The location will vary depending on what's available, your personal style and what you need to do – a quick ten minutes on the bus or at your desk early before anyone's around, or an extended visualization session at home in the evening or perhaps in a quiet church or in a park or in the countryside. The important point is that, although you may not have your idea of the ideal location available, you can try these techniques with whatever time and space you can manage. Many of these approaches, especially as you gain experience through practice, work fine wherever you are, in a few snatched moments: in a quiet café before meeting someone, in the car before a job interview, in an ante-room before you give a presentation.

One last thought on location. If you go somewhere regularly, make a point of seeking out good spaces for a quiet moment or two so that you know where to find them if you feel you need a few moments' rest and peace.

Posture

A comfortable and relaxed posture is important for any kind of relaxation. This can be anything that works for you. You might, if it's possible and suits your style, lie down; the classic relaxation position is good for your body and your mind: head supported so that the neck is not bent (use books), legs drawn in with knees pointing to the ceiling so that the spine is not arched, palms resting either side of the stomach so that the arms are comfortable and relaxed.

If you're sitting down, you need to sit properly, with your spine supported. There's plenty of advice available about the best sitting posture, and some of it is contradictory regarding whether you should have your feet flat on the floor or tucked in behind, for example. Detailed advice is beyond the scope of this book and certainly beyond my competence, but everyone seems to agree that you should avoid sitting for too long and that you should take frequent stretch-breaks. A well-designed and adjustable seat, such as a good office chair, is the ideal, but if this is not available you can achieve a lot if you can manage to get a seat on the train (hear the cries of the occasional commuter!).

Breathing

When you're comfortable, you might like to close your eyes, though this is not essential; focus on your breathing and slowly take deeper and deeper breaths. Take each breath a little deeper so that you are filling your lungs with air, breathing from your diaphragm. You might find it helpful to breathe in to a count of eight, hold for eight, then breathe out for eight and repeat this several times until your breathing becomes deep and regular.

To help you relax as you breathe, you might like to imagine that as you breathe in through your nose you are smelling your favourite flower, or the 'nose' of your favourite wine; and as you breathe out through your mouth you are gently blowing into a candle flame, not to extinguish it but to see it waver in your breath.

Muscles

When you're ready, move on to relaxing your body. Start with your toes and work through your whole body to your head, tensing and relaxing your muscles: toes, ankles, calves, thighs, stomach, fingers, wrists, upper arms, shoulders. Tense and relax each a couple of times. When you get to your face, there are lots of muscles to experiment with, but you might prefer to skip this bit if you're on public transport! All joking aside, our faces do benefit from a muscle workout every so often, so try to find a quiet spot and give them a good stretch. Having a good laugh achieves much the same thing and is more socially acceptable.

Whatever you do, breathing and relaxing, try to enjoy it; you'd pay money for an in-depth relaxation experience and here you can get it for free pretty much whenever you want.

Drifting down

Many people find that some kind of imaginary picture of moving into a deeper, more relaxed state is a useful prelude to further thinking. This might involve imagining that you're walking down a hill or flying gently down or parachuting into a favourite spot or descending a long staircase. Some people find it useful to accompany this with a countdown from ten or twenty. One useful technique is to imagine a meter that records how far you have drifted down into a relaxed state. As you breathe out, imagine that the meter descends another notch or half notch – perhaps there are ten graduations and with each exhalation you see it drop half a unit, starting on ten and descending in stages to zero, which is your fully relaxed state.

A word of warning though: you can also use this technique to help you get to sleep!

You're now ready to undertake your meditation, visualization, writing, thinking or simply enjoying your relaxed state.

2 Body language

We all transmit powerful signals about emotions and thoughts to other people and pick up messages from them in return. Our body language, which we communicate through posture, movement and facial expression, tells people a lot about us and our state of mind and emotions before we even open our mouths.

To illustrate this, try Exercise 2.1. Draw a stick-figure to illustrate the word on the left. Look at my example and then please don't tell me you can't draw!

Exercise 2.1

Scared

Excited

Nervous

Cunning

Confident

Even if you're less than satisfied with your artistic endeavours (and please forgive the suggestion if your drawings are
masterpieces), the fact that you had an idea of what to draw
demonstrates how familiar we all are with the messages our
stances and movements send.

In real life the body communicates in a far more subtle way,
and the first essential to understand is that we are not always
consciously aware of the signals we pick up, but we do receive
and process them at a subconscious level. Have you ever had
the feeling that someone makes you feel uncomfortable, but
you're not sure why? There could be a number of reasons,
ranging from their reminding you of someone with unpleasant
associations, to their sticking a pin in your arm! But it could be
their stance – are they too close to you or do they stand in an
aggressive way, trying to dominate the situation? Conversely, are
they adopting a 'needy' pose, forever looking to you, imploring
some kind of reaction? Any of these things may be happening
but you may not consciously realize that this is so; nevertheless
you feel the responses without knowing the reason for them. If
this is true of the signals you pick up from others, it is doubly
so of the signals you may be sending out without realizing it,

and so a rudimentary understanding of and sensitivity to body language can be valuable when working on your confidence.

For Exercise 2.2, I want you to think about a situation in which you feel unconfident and write down some thoughts about your body language in that situation. There's an example first.

Exercise 2.2

When I had to talk to a large group of people.	As I walked on to the platform my head was down. I shuffled as I spoke. At one or two points I put my hand over my mouth as I was speaking. I felt uncomfortable being there and I'm sure it affected what I said and how the audience perceived me and, more importantly, what they took away about my important message.

Changing your stance and movement

In the example above, the body language is unhelpful, it doesn't put others at their ease and is likely to lead them to be distracted. But once we understand the power of these unspoken messages it becomes possible to change them into something more positive, more confidence-building. So, continuing with the above example, if you have to appear confident in front of others, and it can be just one person not a roomful as in this example, how can you change the situation through adjusting your stance and movement?

The answer is to break things down into simple steps that you can work on.

'My head was down'

Practise walking with your head up.

If you can see the space beforehand, find something at about the right height in the room that you can look at as you walk, but don't become an automaton and ignore people – make eye contact (see below) as you enter a small meeting and, of course, you can look down to make sure you don't trip! The trick is to think, 'look up at the picture' or whatever it is you have in mind, so that you don't spend most of the journey looking down and thus appearing unconfident.

Another tip about confident upright posture that I still use in my acting classes, though it's as old as the hills, is to imagine an invisible string running through your spine and head, pulling you upright like a marionette. It does seem to work!

'I shuffled as I spoke'

A little movement is natural, but you can make a big difference to how people perceive you by practising a couple of confident poses and alternating between them as you speak. A confident pose would be one with your feet slightly apart and your body comfortably upright, your hands hanging naturally to your sides when relaxed but ready to support what you say when appropriate. Use your hands to add emphasis and also to offer you alternative poses, such as one hand on a lectern – or occasionally bring your hands together. Over time you can train yourself to be aware but not overly self-conscious of your hands, and use them to aid your confidence and communication skills.

My colleague at the Actors Centre in Business, Mark Bowden, has developed an effective technique based on different body zones, which he calls the Gesture-Plane System: let your hands hang below your belly button as you speak (the Grotesque-Plane) and the effect is downbeat; bring them to stomach or belly-button level (the Truth-Plane) and use them expressively there and the effect is positive but not overbearing; raise them higher to chest level (the Passion-Plane) and your voice follows them up and you seem excited but perhaps not overly so. Experiment for yourself and see if you can train your hands to find the right zone to give you confidence. There's a lot more to this, and as you can learn a lot from having a go in a supportive environment you might want to check out Mark's workshops at <www.actorscentreinbusiness.co.uk>.

For sitting, lean slightly forward as you speak and listen to show interest and involvement; don't cross your arms for extended periods as this can send out a 'blocking' signal; and once you've found a comfortable and open position, try not to change it too often – the fidgets are offputting.

'I put my hand over my mouth as I was speaking'

This is a definite no-no if you want to appear confident. The hand in front of the mouth suggests that you don't want your words to reach others and sends a negative signal about you.

Identify the hand that is most likely to do this and hold something in it – some notes, an illustrative object or a pencil, for example. Or imagine that you are holding something. If this imaginary approach sounds bizarre, it works by helping you to be aware of the movement: as you lift your arm you think, 'That's my stick-holding hand' and this thought triggers you to stop the movement. Any activity that helps you to be aware of the 'phantom blocking-hand' will help. If there's a lectern, put the offending hand on it, which will ensure that you're aware as it moves towards your mouth. Another tip is to ensure that you mostly keep your palms forward as you speak – it's an open gesture that speaks of relaxed confidence, and it prevents you from clenching your hands, which sends a less positive message.

All this talk of offending hands reminds me of the horror movie where someone's hand has a life of its own and ends up strangling the 'hero'. A bit extreme? Surely it's not that far removed from your mouth saying one thing and your body shouting out loud and clear 'He doesn't really mean it' or 'Liar, liar'!

Practise, practise

You may well be thinking at this point, 'So I'm not very confident anyway and I've got to talk to this group or meet this individual and now I've got a notebook to keep hold of and a stance to keep up and another to have ready and something on the wall to look at and a pair of misbehaving hands to keep under control – and this is supposed to make me *more* confident!

This is a fair point and the answer is simple: practise. If you were giving a speech you'd practise; if you were learning a dance you'd practise – so why not practise your stance? There's nothing dumb about practising how to enter a room to create the right impression. It's the kind of thing I do with delegates on Trainer Training and Confidence courses all the time. If you're ever in our house before I have to deliver a course, you might catch me wandering around mumbling and gesticulating to myself – it's practice and it's far better to learn to get your body language right before the big day than to get it wrong when it really matters. If you can, and the occasion warrants it, why not get a friend or trusted colleague in to look at your talk or practise your interview with you, and ask them to pay particular attention to your body language. Like everything in this book, it's not about a sprinkling of magic life-changing confidence powder but about practical steps you can take that will make a real difference.

And there's one other key message here: awareness is a kind of doing. What this means is that simply by reading about and reflecting on body language, you will become more aware and thus more able to work positively with the signals you send out. If you know about putting your hand in front of your mouth, for example, you're less likely to do it.

Body language on the phone!

Everything I've said above also applies when you're on the phone. Even if you can't be seen, your stance will affect how you sound, so when you need to be assertive and sound confident on the phone, stand up tall, lift your head and be positive! It's so much more likely to get results than slouching and mumbling.

Understanding the signals

As I write this I'm thinking about a recent planning event that I attended for some creativity work I'm leading. There were four of us around a table and I sat on the same side as someone I'll call Toni. The meeting was really buzzy and we got a lot done. We were on track to finish about an hour early, which I could tell we all thought was fine, but then, as so often happens, there was a reluctance to finish – a couple of things were revisited and a few practical points were raised. Of the four of us, only I could see Toni's feet, and her right foot was going nineteen to the dozen, flipping up and down in the air as she sat cross-legged. I knew the signal at once: tapping or bouncing feet are the body's way of saying, 'Let's go'. The person doing this has had enough; they're ready to move on (although they may not necessarily be consciously aware of this) and so their feet and legs are already in motion. It's a signal to watch out for and there are many more. Table 2.1 gives some suggestions for how to interpret certain body language signals – but remember that it's not an exact science, and that you may find different interpretations elsewhere.

Table 2.1 Interpreting body language

Action	Meaning
Legs or feet tapping or waving	'Let's go'
Arms folded	Defensive
Hands on head	Mild aggression – I'm making my body big
Rubbing the back of the head (or anywhere!)	Uncertain or frustrated
Sitting with feet pointing inwards	Not confident in the situation
Sitting with legs apart, hands on thighs, feet pointing outwards	Very confident, open, can also imply superiority
Looking away and around the room	Uninterested
Hand moving to face while speaking	Unsure of self, of the truth of what you're saying or of how others will perceive it
Standing with hands on hips	Dominant, aggressive
Stroking stomach	In need of comfort
Standing with hands clasped	Less confident
In constant motion, from foot to foot, for example	Nervous

There are many more of these 'tells' (actions and movements that betray our true thoughts and feelings) but I want to add an important word of caution. In any group you will undoubtedly find various forms of these kinds of body language. If you're talking to a group of, say, four people for any length of time, someone will at one point look around as if bored; someone else will adopt a slightly aggressive pose and so on. This just happens in groups because no one can stay focused in one mode for long periods of time. We all have 'off-line time' when we're not really 'in the moment', when our thoughts have drifted, and these lead to changes in posture and expression. The trick is not to be put off by these. Unconfident thinking would be, 'Frank's looking bored; I must be rubbish; I'm sure they're all feeling the same'; confident thinking would be, 'Frank's looking bored but he might be being thoughtful. If he doesn't look interested in a while, I'll change tack and perhaps have a chat with him later.' Perspective can help us to achieve our goals by seeing that not everything that happens is a response to us and that we do not have to magnify every situation into a drama.

Eye contact

Before leaving body language, I want to say something about eye contact, because our eyes are a 'window on the soul' and because how others perceive us is greatly influenced by what they 'see in our eyes'. What signals do you pick up from these eye contact scenarios given in Exercise 2.3?

Exercise 2.3

Looking down at the ground	
Not making eye contact	
Making and then immediately breaking eye contact	
Making prolonged and unblinking eye contact	
Eyes constantly sweeping the room	
Constantly looking up	

Eyebrows and forehead furrowed	
Winking	
Closing eyes for periods during conversation	
Blinking	

Exercise 2.3 is not a 'right or wrong' exercise, although many people will have similar reactions to these eye contact scenarios and body language lore has some firm ideas about each of them. The important point is how you perceive each one, and the idea is to get you thinking about what you see in people's eyes and what they see in yours. But there's a further important point, which is that none of these states is right or wrong for the duration of a meeting or conversation. There will be times when someone you're talking to might look around or up or down, and you needn't be too sensitive to it as a signal. Each of these only really becomes important when it happens a lot, so almost constant looking down would be a good indicator of nervousness or reluctance to engage; prolonged contact might be an indication that the speaker has a strong interest in getting their message across and wants you to keep looking at them (this could be for negative reasons – like someone who is determined that their view should dominate – or it could be the look of an enraptured lover).

Here's my version of what's going on with the eye contact scenarios in Exercise 2.3.

Looking down at the ground	Unconfident, nervous, reluctant to engage ... or lost an earring!
Not making eye contact	Unconfident, overawed, bored ... or just plain rude!
Making and then immediately breaking eye contact	Unconfident, uncertain of the situation ... or eating lunch!
Making prolonged and unblinking eye contact	Extremely interested ... or extremely overbearing!
Eyes constantly sweeping the room	Want to go, looking for someone else ... or a bad and rather obvious spy!
Constantly looking up	Mind on higher things ... or an astronomer!
Eyebrows and forehead furrowed	Deep in thought, considering what you say ... or a Neanderthal!
Winking	Sending a message such as, 'I don't mean what I say' or 'I fancy you' ... or sand in eye!
Closing eyes for periods during conversation	Thoughtful ... or sleepy, prayerful!
Blinking	Nervous, have a tic ... or staring at bright light!

So not all eye movements mean the same things for all people in all circumstances. Like all body language, it's not an exact science – but our eyes do reveal a lot, and the best course of action is to be as natural as you can, because if you try to cover things up, your eyes will often betray you. But what if you find the whole idea of making eye contact challenging? I have one tip that a number of people have found helpful: look at the person's eyebrows rather than their eyes – it has the same direct effect but is much easier to maintain if you're feeling at all uncomfortable.

Try to avoid a 'dead smile', one that moves your facial muscles in the right ways but leaves your eyes lacking conviction. It can be helpful to think positive and use your imagination to put you in a positive and happy frame of mind, so think about your loved ones, perhaps a child running towards you with arms outstretched, or a friend who you're always delighted to see.

This has been a brief dip into the fascinating area of body language and its connections with confidence. I have a book to recommend for further reading: *Body Language at Work* by Mary Hartley (Sheldon Press, 2003). It's full of terrific insight and advice about body language in general, alongside work-related advice, exercises and case studies. Another good one is *The Definitive Book of Body Language: How to Read Others' Attitudes by Their Gestures* by Allan and Barbara Pease (Orion, 2005) – a best-selling classic.

3 Appearance

People form their first impressions of us within the very first seconds of meeting us. They form ideas about us based on how we look, how we're dressed and the signals we give off through our posture and facial expressions (see previous section, 'Body language'). Exercise 2.4 is designed to reveal how much we base our impressions on our first sight of other people.

You need a newspaper or magazine for Exercise 2.4, preferably one you haven't looked at before. Open it at random and find some pictures of people; look at one person for five seconds then close the paper and fill in the exercise.

Exercise 2.4

Male or female?	
Age?	

Salary range?	
How much do they care about their appearance?	
How would you describe their clothing style?	
Do you and this person have much in common?	
Name three dominant characteristics of this individual.	
What do you envy about this person?	
What could they learn from you?	
Would you like to get to know them?	
Would you trust this person?	
Write down any words that come to mind when you look at this person.	

Of course, Exercise 2.4 is just an exercise and there are a number of reasons why it might not match a real-life situation: the photograph may have been selected or carefully staged by the publisher to create a particular impression; it may have been touched up to convey a message (particularly but not exclusively applicable to adverts); it may be of someone you recognize, such as a celebrity or politician whose image is already familiar to you. Nevertheless, a simple exercise like this can reveal how many assumptions we make based on how people look. These early impressions can be surprisingly tenacious and difficult to shake off. Get off on the wrong foot with someone and it can take a long time to put this in the past and form a more constructive relationship.

However, I should stress that first impressions are not indelible. It is possible to think again and move on. But given that these first impressions are important, how can we use this knowledge to our advantage? The key lies in one word: confidence. This may be unsurprising in the context of this book, but as we saw in the section on body language, confident behaviour, in this case having confidence in your appearance, is the key to getting off on the right foot in any situation. There are two linked areas to think about here: face and clothes.

Face

Our faces are incredibly important to us; they define us to a large extent – just think of how the word is used: face the facts, face the future, face it, face to face and so on. These reveal our understanding that our faces represent our essence when meeting challenges. Then there are the ways we refer to other people's faces, often in a derogatory fashion – phrases like 'She/He's got a face like a (insert derogatory term)'; 'If looks could kill'; 'Why the miserable face?' Faces are terribly important in how we communicate with the world, or how we inter*face*. I've produced a lot of radio drama in my time and also trained many people as radio producers and drama directors. As an actor and director I love radio, partly because I can ignore what I and others look like, which opens up great possibilities in casting. Indeed, one of the classes I teach at the London and Manchester Actors Centres is called 'radio cross-dressing', the idea being that if you can sound like it, you can be it! One course participant told me that he'd bought his wife a book about the long-running UK radio serial drama, *The Archers*. She'd been thrilled, being a big fan, but had said to him, 'Before I look at it, darling, would you go through and put a Post-it note over any pictures of the actors?' She had her own idea of what the characters looked like and didn't want to be swayed by the actual faces of the cast. There's a radio broadcaster I won't name who's often on BBC radio, and his voice sounds decidedly sinister to me – it gives me the shivers whenever I hear it and, based on his voice alone, I wouldn't trust him very far. Yet meet him or see him on TV and you don't get this impression at all. All the sinister qualities that I thought I heard are just not there, rather his face and voice together give an impression of someone thoughtful and trustworthy. So while as a radio writer and producer I'd never play down the importance of how we sound, I do think that our faces often speak just as loud as our voices.

What can we do about our faces, though? After all, we're pretty much stuck with them, aren't we? That's an interesting question, because if you look at it a little more deeply it poses a more profound one: why would you want to change your face? Perhaps you don't, but many people do, as the worldwide multi-billion dollar cosmetics industry demonstrates with, of course, a particular focus on women. I'm not revealing anything startling when I say that people are led, or manipulated if you prefer, to consider 'improving' their faces by an image of a particular kind of beauty to which they are encouraged to aspire. Let's explore this with Exercise 2.5.

Exercise 2.5: Face-rating exercise

Take some time to look around and, if possible, gather images of the kind of face you'd like to aspire to. To do this exercise properly you need to put aside the kind of doublethink that we all engage in along the lines of:

Think: 'I wish I looked like her/him.'

Doublethink: 'That's a shallow way to be; I mustn't think like that.'
Think: 'Yes, but I *do* wish I looked like her/him.'

Put aside what you know about how you're being manipulated and led down certain paths by celebrity image and advertising – just go for the initial first impression and see if, after your research, you can come up with a brief statement:

'The face I'd like is...'

You may simply write: 'The face I'd like is the one I've got'; or you might write something like: 'The face I'd like is the one I've got but with a better-shaped nose', or 'The face I'd like is the one that Xxxxxx has.'

Does Exercise 2.5 reveal that you are dissatisfied with your face?

How would you rate this dissatisfaction on a scale of one (very satisfied) to ten (very dissatisfied)? We'll come back to this result at the end of this section.

We can't talk about faces in our culture without mentioning cosmetic surgery – an expensive lifestyle choice in a world where basic medicine is not available to the majority; it could even be argued that in many cases it is a misuse of medical training, expertise and resources. I exempt from this those with facial or other disfigurement that prevent them living a normal life, though even in this circumstance some people choose not to have surgery and to say to the world, 'This is who I am and I'm happy with it.' I think these people offer an interesting balance to our norm-obsessed world.

If you're a woman you may well be thinking at this point, 'What does he know about it; it's different for women? There are far greater pressures on us to conform to societal norms about looks: appearance has a far greater effect on women's job prospects, to take just one example.'

I hold my hands up and say, 'You're right'; but I do, in fact, have something to say about this that's relevant to all, both men and women. It's a personal story and it taps right into our central theme of confidence.

I was born with a vivid red birthmark (port wine stain) on the left temple. In adulthood it gradually became purpler in colour and thus stood out even more. Of course I was teased and made fun of at school, but this didn't seem to stop me pursuing my career – as a teacher, director, actor and writer, then later as a BBC producer and, since 2001, as a freelancer with a variety of jobs, including the very face-to-face business of training and development. It didn't stop the woman I love marrying me (though this says more about her qualities than mine), and it didn't stop me being part of the family that is my bedrock. However, when I began to do more training work, I started to think about looking into the possibility of getting something done about my birthmark because I recognized the issue we're exploring here: that people form quick impressions, and I didn't want training delegates to be puzzling over my face at our first meeting. This, of course, became even more important when I started acting. I saw my doctor, who recommended me to the dermatology unit at a London hospital. To cut a long story short, there were various options and I took the camouflage make-up route. So now, every morning, I mix my two shades to get the right match for my skin colour and apply it to part of my face to make my birthmark disappear – with, it must be said, varying degrees of success depending on the hour of the morning and the activities of the night before. So, female readers, if you're one of those who say that you can't face the world without your make-up (or wack as we call it in this house), I'm with you.

Bridget
A member of the Birthmark Support Group <www.btinternet.com/~birthmarksupportgroup/home.htm>, Bridget Crawshaw has a similar story from a woman's perspective. Here's what she says about how her face affects her confidence:

'Confidence is a strange thing. I have certain situations where I feel "safe" and others where I will run a mile if possible.
    'I have a birthmark on the right side of my face which was operated

on over a period of time, and I've been left with a scar. My husband has given me a great deal of confidence and most days now I wear normal foundation all over my face (unless I'm in the house and not going out), but on the days when I feel a bit self-conscious I put an extra dollop of thicker foundation over the scar and birthmark. I used to wear the really thick camouflage make-up and spent hours dotting on freckles! I had laser treatment a few years ago, which took away a lot of the redness, so it's easier to cover now. My husband has times when he can't understand how I feel, but finds it endearing when I have to rearrange furniture in restaurants (I find it more difficult to sit opposite than next to him). He says he thinks it takes more confidence to rearrange the furniture under the glaring eyes of waiters!

'I find all formal situations stressful, even meals with my immediate family – there was one particular incident at a hospital check-up when I was little that is imprinted on my mind: I remember being called in to see the plastic surgeon, and when I walked in there he was the behind his desk and behind him was a row of trainees. It was awful. I endured the usual prodding and poking and was stared at by all these people. I can't remember whether we were even given the option of whether we wanted them there or not, or even how many there were, but to a small child and in my mind now there were too many!

This may seem insignificant to some but each time I was in hospital, and the team of doctors would come round to look, I wanted to curl up and die.

'I am certain that that day has had a big impact on my behaviour. I think up to a point when you are little you are oblivious, and your parents are going through hell, and then you become aware that things are not exactly how they should be!

'Now if I've been in a doctor's surgery or wherever and I get asked if I mind students being present, I say "Yes" and ask them to leave (but then feel bad!).'

Bridget has gone through the stages of becoming aware of her face, feeling that it is 'different', then working on strategies to deal with this, including surgery but also the 'Where I sit' approach. Also of interest is the 'hospital incident' where one single event has had a big effect on her. Another big factor is the support of her husband and her parents. Her confidence is not a 'constant' but she shows considerable healthy assertiveness in saying 'No' when asked if students can be present; she feels bad about it afterwards but this simply demonstrates her sensitivity to others, an attitude that has not always been shown to her.

In both Bridget's and my own case, we do feel more confident now, more able to face the world; I no longer worry about standing out as 'different' in a negative way; for Bridget there are times when she still feels uncomfortable but she has the classic approach explored in this book: she takes things one by one and finds strategies to cope rather than let her feelings rule her life.

Another interesting thing that I've learnt is that my birthmark always mattered more to me than it did to other people. It's clear that some friends and acquaintances don't remember that I once had this mark, or they remember only vaguely. It's quite amusing to me when I see people I haven't seen for a while and they say things like, 'You look well'; something is different but they can't quite figure what it is. Other comments were, 'Have you stopped wearing glasses?' and 'There's something different about you – have you had a haircut?' These tell me that they never noticed my mark much; it was just part, but by no means the dominant part, of the whole picture of 'me'. Another amusing aspect is that if I get the make-up mix wrong and it comes out too red, people say 'You've caught the sun!' So I just smile or say that I went to sleep in the garden – this doesn't work so well in the most common type of English weather, of course!

I wonder what lessons you draw from these stories. Do they give the lie to my comments on cosmetic surgery – Gordon (that's me) has gained confidence by changing his face, so why can't Jane or Mahinda do the same by changing the shape of their noses? Does it make you think that the way we see ourselves is not how others see us? Does it make you think that presenting an attractive face to the world is a matter of confidence?

You'll not be surprised to read that I believe the last two

points are the ones to take further, if for no other reason than that I'm not in a position to give you make-up or plastic surgery advice but I have learnt that it was my confidence that needed boosting, not my physicality. Yes, the one fed the other and, yes, people do form first impressions based on appearance. But appearance is more than 'nature given'; it's about animation, life, vitality, warmth – and these all orbit around c_____e (fill in the missing word and give yourself a prize!).

Boosting facial confidence

Have you ever met someone you found engaging, personable and attractive to look at and be with, but who didn't conform to any of your stereotypes of facial attractiveness – someone of whom you might say that her personality shone through, or that he seemed so alive? If so, you'll understand that physical attractiveness, whatever we mean by that, is related to confident behaviour – it is exhibited by people who feel 'comfortable in their skin', who are happy to be who they are. So does this mean, after a few hundred words about faces, that they don't matter? I don't believe this is the right conclusion to draw. People do respond to our faces – of course they do – but as well as responding to 'what God or fate gave us' (our bone structure, hair, skin, eye colour, lip shape and all the other things that go to make up our current idea of an attractive face), people also respond to how our faces convey our personality, and there are certain things we can do to be more confident about our faces.

1 *Gain perspective.* It's that central theme of this book again! Learn to see that others don't see your face as you do. They'll be far less critical and negative than you. Your face is not a barrier to them, though what you do with it may be if you scowl and look askance at people.
2 *Prepare to meet the world.* If having your hair a certain way and putting on make-up is important to you, admit this

and allow time for it. See it as a kind of ritual, like an actor preparing their make-up and costume before meeting their audience, but be aware that this is a ritual that you choose – don't become a slave to it. Can you be really confident and, just occasionally, face the world without going through this preparation, as Bridget has begun to do?

3 *Exercise your face.* There are 44 muscles in the human face – more than any other animal – so it's a good idea to give them a workout every so often. You can simply try stretching and relaxing as many facial muscles as you can – the shower or bath is good for this as long as you don't open wide under the gushing stream. Singing is good or – one that actors often use – imagine chewing a piece of gum that as you chew grows larger and larger until you're really stretching your mouth.

Try some tongue-twisters, such as, 'Red Lorry, Yellow Lorry' or its evil twin, 'Red Lorry, Yellow Lorry, Red Leather, Yellow Leather'; 'Unique New York' or my particular bête noire, 'Peggy Babcock'. These will give your mouth, lips and many face muscles a good workout.

If you can, give your face a quick workout before you enter the situation in which you need to feel confident – if nothing else, wrestling with Peggy Babcock will take your mind off what's to come!

4 Lauren Bacall said, 'I think your whole life shows in your face and you should be proud of that.' What is the life story your face tells? Write or think about your own version of this:

This is the face that formed and grew in the womb.
This is the face that brought me my first breath, my first smell, sight, sound and taste of the world.
This is the face that tasted home cooking.
This is the face that I offered to my lover.
This is the face that welcomed my children.

… and so on.

If you like you can use Exercise 2.6 to help. Use any of the categories that you find useful and make up your own too.

Exercise 2.6

This is the face that ...	(something from childhood)
This is the face that ...	(something from your parents)
This is the face that ...	(something from your relations)
This is the face that ...	(something from your friends)
This is the face that ...	(something from an important relationship)
This is the face that ...	(something you have seen)
This is the face that ...	(something you have heard)
This is the face that ...	(something you have smelled – a memory, triggered by a smell?)
This is the face that ...	(something you have tasted)
This is the face that ...	(something(s) unique and special to you)

Your face has been your portal to the world and your offering to the world throughout your whole life – it hasn't done too badly, has it? You may say that this isn't the face that did all those things because it has grown and changed, but this is part of the story: our faces change as we do; they grow as we do and they reflect our changing, growing lives.

By far the most important thing about our faces is the message they send out about us, not 'See how lucky I am to have been born with this beauty' or 'See how using make-up and hairdressing I have made the most of what I have' but 'This is who I am, open, generous, fun-loving, loving...'

After thinking about these things, go back to the face-rating exercise earlier in this section – how satisfied are you with your face now? And what is your strategy for becoming more confident still in how you look?

Clothes

We tend to think about how our clothing makes us appear to the world, how it makes us stand out or fit in, what 'message' it sends, such as 'I am professional, relaxed, sexy, pragmatic or indifferent.' There are plenty of books and television programmes that take the approach of 'a new you through new clothes', but I want to stress that the most important thing about the clothes we wear is not the effect they have on others, but how they make us feel, and following on from this, how they can boost our confidence. The two sides of the coin are linked, of course (it would be a strange coin if they weren't): feeling confident about how others see us affects how we feel about ourselves, but I think it's essential to put ourselves first and not simply conform because everyone else does. Having said that, I think it would be fair to suggest that for most adolescents, these approaches do not apply. Many feel that they have to conform to this year's, month's, week's, day's or even minute's fashion for their culture, subculture or even microculture, for fear of getting picked on or bullied. There is also a pervasive and often pernicious value-judgement process for many young people concerning branding. It takes confidence to ignore the overpriced, well-marketed labels, and buy what you want rather than what they are telling you you need.

We should also recognize that most adults will still carry these urges to conform within them, but perhaps as adults we can work with them rather than be ruled by them.

Clothes are multifaceted, having characteristics of:

- practicality: an apron or a swimming costume, for example
- sexual allure: how much does this cover up or reveal and how provocatively?
- body shaping: plenty of underwear options, mostly, but not exclusively, for women
- directing attention: the colour or detail that draws the eye, the hat that shouts 'Look at me'
- protecting from the elements: a thick jumper, a waterproof coat, a sun hat
- identification: a uniform such as a police officer's, a nurse's, a fast-food restaurant worker's
- works of art: couture
- disguise: costume for a play, for example
- carriers: pockets for small change etc.
- tradition: a tie (what is that scrap of material for?), a kilt, a grass skirt
- sexual display: *that's* what a tie is for!
- modesty: anything that covers any part of the body we are not comfortable with showing.

Try Exercise 2.7. Take a look at three items of clothing you have worn recently and, using the categories above, ask yourself what functions they have and then what messages they send to others. I've given a couple of examples.

Exercise 2.7

Item	Functions	Messages
Cheap shorts	Protect from elements: keep me cool in heatwave Carriers: pockets for keys, cash, wallet	Casual, not concerned about looks, slightly scruffy, practical. They clearly say, 'It's hot and that's the most important thing at the moment'
Cream jacket	Protect from elements: maintains a good balance of coolness in sun but protection from colder night air Carriers: pockets for keys, phone etc. Tradition: conveys a certain low-key respectability, important for the person I'm visiting	Wearer has thought about appearance and wants to suggest a casual but not downbeat style
(Add your own below)		

Now the important part: how did wearing the clothes make you feel? Did they feel appropriate to you, to the situation, and thus increase your confidence? We've all heard stories of people arriving for events wearing 'inappropriate' clothes: you're in fancy dress and no one else is, or your dress is over-formal for a dinner party, or you're the only one not wearing a tie. In most cases wearing 'the wrong thing' merely means being different from everyone else. Admittedly, if you turn up to fish without waders when everyone else has them, you're going to be at a disadvantage; similarly, if you have sweaty clothes on when everyone else is dressed for the hot sun, you're going to be in some difficulties. But in the scheme of things, does it really matter if you've got the 'right colour for the season' or 'black tie'? In my view, people who insist on such things ought to get a life, as life is too short to be obsessed by style and conforming to other people's norms. I went to a garden party at Buckingham Palace without wearing a tie and I was in excellent company as about half the people there were similarly tieless. They were all women, of course, but I figured if it's good enough for the queen...

I'm also in good company since James Dyson, the vacuum-cleaner entrepreneur, said of ties in a *Daily Telegraph* article in June 2000: 'They are ridiculous things, entirely to do with convention.' And he's overtaken many a besuited executive with his creative thinking.

Feeling confident about our clothes can be expressed in the following ways:

- confident that I'll fit in or stand out to the extent that I want to;
- confident that I'll be physically comfortable in these clothes;
- confident that I won't be banned for what I wear or confident that I want that confrontation;
- confident that the clothes are appropriate for the event/task;
- confident in the message that these clothes send out about me.

Some people feel a lack of confidence about shopping for clothes, so how can all this translate into practice when choosing or buying clothes? We'll focus on buying the clothes as a way of exploring some practical ideas – and thanks to my women friends for their help with this bit.

The first essential is clarity of purpose: what are the clothes for; what functions will they serve – as explored earlier in this section. One useful preliminary to a shopping trip is to put on something that you feel comfortable wearing and that gives you a feeling of confidence, then ask yourself why it works – is it the cut, the style, the material, the comfort factor? Use this under-standing to help you as you shop for new clothes.

You also need to have confidence in the clothes as in the list of confidences above.

Take time to plan a good opportunity to go shopping. You're looking for a time that suits you, perhaps a quieter spot in a busy shopping day if you can manage it; or you could of course shop online, again taking your time and being crystal clear about your aims.

If you can, find a shop you feel comfortable in, where you can ask for advice. Pick your time well and you'll find that the assistants will be delighted to take some trouble over you if they've spent too long standing around. There are personal shoppers who can help in some stores, but again, you must take control by knowing what you want and conveying it clearly and firmly.

Practise a confident posture when you try on clothes (see Section 2, 'Body language') and try to imagine all the different ways you will use them – sit, stand, reach; whatever's appropriate. If there is any discomfort you need to make a judgement about whether it will get worse with time (an hour of this sticking in me will be agony) or better (it'll stretch after a few wears).

You might like to take a trusted friend with you and brief them in advance on your aims.

Take or wear the right underwear and shoes when shopping – you'll find it harder to buy a business suit if you're not wearing the right bra, or have flip-flops on your feet.

But doesn't all this planning and forethought take the fun out of shopping? Isn't the whole adventure about that unexpected, 'so right for me' bargain just around the corner? After all, if you enjoy shopping for clothes, who'd want to take that away from you? Yet it can only be good to know in advance what you're aiming for in terms of the confidence you feel when wearing your purchases. Even if you only know it so you can choose to ignore it!

Finally, if you find yourself uncertain – 'Do I want this or not?' 'Do I want that or the other?' – use the well-known trick of picking two options and tossing a coin. Note how you feel when, for example, heads come up for that black dress. Pleased? Then go ahead and buy. Disappointed? Put it back on the rack. Confused? You're not ready to commit yet – come back later. The tossing of the coin isn't about letting luck decide for you, it's about noting your reactions and using these as a guide.

4 Feelings, thoughts and core beliefs

There's a well-known relationship that underpins much counselling and coaching, namely the connection between feelings, thoughts and beliefs. In a nutshell, it goes like this: our feelings are a response to our thoughts and our thoughts come from our beliefs; so if we can identify, understand and modify those core beliefs we all have about ourselves, we can change our thinking, our feelings and our behaviour – we can take more control of our lives.

In this section there are practical exercises, with two versions of each – one to be undertaken if you have the time and space to write down your thoughts, the other taking a more meditative approach for when you're on a journey, out for a walk or relaxing in the bath. As well as their practical implications (space and time to write mainly), each set of exercises has a different focus to suit different learning styles. In general the thinking versions are more imaginative and the written ones more pragmatic. It's best to read both before starting either as you may find that a combination suits you best or that, being the creative person you are, you develop your own approach as a synthesis of the two.

Remember: if it looks like a lot of work and 'too heavy', just take what you want and work with that. Often the explanation takes up more time than the actual exercise and you'll probably find that much of the thinking can go on in the background as you do other things.

My experience

As I got started on this book I was also doing something I'd never done before: beta testing a piece of software. I thought that the variety of doing something different would be a good refreshing counterpoint to the writing. Beta testing is the process of weeding out bugs and suggesting improvements before the software is published. Volunteers try it out and usually receive a free copy of the published programme in return. This software was the latest version of a programme I used regularly and I was asked to participate after posting some comments on the publisher's open forum. One day I found myself in one of those 'I'm doing everything right – why won't you work!' type of situations. If you've ever shouted at a computer, you're with me.

I want to try to recreate here, in all its embarrassing and unconfident detail, what I was thinking over the hour or so that I struggled with this.

I began with some enthusiasm because I'd been having problems with part of the programme for a while; here was the ideal opportunity to sort this out, gain some clarity on the problem and contribute in a helpful way to the beta testing process at the same time. I'll spare you the tedious details, but I gradually became more and more frustrated as I couldn't get it to do what I wanted. Frustration at this sort of thing is a natural and helpful reaction; it's a sign that it's time to step back, reassess and decide what to try next – more experimentation or perhaps it's time to phone a friend, in this case call a helpline or post a message on the beta testers' forum, where people are generally helpful and supportive. Instead of following this reflective course of action, one I've often advocated in print and on courses, I allowed the frustration to feed a generalization and, embarrassingly stupid as it sounds, it went something like this: I bet no one else is having this problem; they'll all be on top of it; I'm just not very good at this sort of thing; I'm getting too old and my mind isn't as sharp as it was; I'm pretty useless at the moment.

I know! It's a ridiculous and pathetic response to a little problem, but there's worse: that morning I'd been doing my accounts for the last three months and my monthly average was a bit down on the same period in the previous year. Despite knowing the reasons for this and accepting that this is the nature of freelance working (the feast or famine principle known to all freelancers), I'd filed it away at the back of my mind to be pulled out and added to the monologue of failure – when the software problems started. So now I was enfeebled with a rapidly deteriorating mind, and the proof was there for all to see in my downward-sliding earning capacity!

Those, then, were my thoughts, but accompanying them was a set of feelings: gloominess and despondency and a solid-feeling lump in my stomach (there's more on locating our feelings later on, in Section 5 of this chapter, 'Visualization'). It was as though I'd taken a paranoia pill and everything was out to do me down.

It goes without saying that the above is not an example of confident behaviour and that it fits better under the category of making a drama out of a stray thought or two. If you've never played this game of seeing things through negative specs and lumping all the bad ingredients together to make the cake of doom, sincere congratulations, but I'm willing to bet that most people will have undertaken this negative role-play at some time, and many will recognize it as a regular part of the repertoire of their 'mind theatre'; and when we stir a bit of overactive exaggeration into the mix it makes us feel rotten and doesn't help us or anyone else in the slightest. So why does it happen? Why do we, sometimes at the slightest opportunity, jump into bed and cuddle up with our negative self-image?

The belief connection

As mentioned above, our feelings are a response to our thoughts:

Feeling	Thought
positive, happy, enthusiastic	I'm so lucky to have this great family around me
uncertain, nervous, scared and perhaps determined	I wonder how hard the exam's going to be
resentment, anger, resignation, perhaps determination	I've got to clean the house before tonight
self-doubt, feelings of worthlessness, sadness	My date hasn't called back; I don't think (s)he will
pleasure, accomplishment, feelings of value and self-belief	That's not a bad website I've designed

And our thoughts grow out of our core beliefs:

Thought	Core belief
I'm so lucky to have this great family around me	I value family; family love and togetherness is a good thing; it is to be celebrated
I wonder how hard the exam's going to be	I find the unknown disturbing; I am uncertain of my abilities

I've got to clean the house before tonight	I have duties; there are things I should do even if I don't want to
My date hasn't called back; I don't think (s)he will	I'm not good on dates; I don't relate well to (wo)men
That's not a bad website I've designed	I have creative ability and I can take pleasure in using it

We all have core beliefs about ourselves, and these beliefs inform what we think, say and feel, so the first stage in working on this is to examine the core beliefs that have informed our thoughts and our feelings. But before we go any further I want to re-emphasize my own core belief about finding practical ways forward, ways to deal more confidently with a given situation. It's perfectly possible, when exploring core beliefs, to focus on where they come from and trace them to specific instances, often in our childhood, but this is not an approach I'm interested in here. As with so much else in this book, I want us to find positive and realistic steps that we can take as a result of our discoveries.

Exercise 2.8a: Core beliefs – Written

To begin working on this, draw up a table like the one below and see if you can start to make connections between your feelings and the thoughts that give rise to them.

   If you find it difficult to fill in the columns, allow yourself some thinking time. Once you are in a relaxed state and ready to reflect, go back over the events of the day, or yesterday, and dwell for a few moments on each one, asking yourself: 'What was my attitude?' 'What was I feeling?' 'What was I thinking?' You only need to come up with one or two examples, but a few more would help to extend the range of ideas to work on.

Feeling	Thought

When you've filled in the table in Exercise 2.8a, it might be a good idea to leave the exercise for a while before returning to it, in order to let your thoughts settle and be 'processed', or try 2.8b if you prefer.

Exercise 2.8b: Core beliefs – Thinking

This is a version of the above that you can do without writing equipment:

1 Read the instructions for the written version and do the thinking to establish the key events of the day.
2 Choose one incident and focus on the feelings it engendered.
3 Create a mental image of the feeling(s), see it as a colour, an animal or anything that represents its qualities.

4 Imagine that the (representation of) the feeling is gradually growing trans-
   parent, and through it you begin to see the thoughts that gave rise to it,
   written as text or quotes in speech bubbles. If you see many thoughts,
   pick one or two to remember for working on in the next phase.

When you're ready, move on to filling in a second table in
Exercise 2.9a (see page 51), this time putting the thoughts you
arrived at in Exercise 2.8a on the left-hand side and the core
beliefs that triggered them on the right.

It can be quite challenging sometimes to relate thoughts to
core beliefs, and I think this is in part due to the fact that our
beliefs are so intrinsic, so much part of us that we find it difficult
to turn around and look at them, to isolate and identify them.
Again, some time for thinking will help, and perhaps the following example will aid this:

I wrote above about the idea of leaving something for a while – I
call it 'refrain' in the Quintessence creative thinking programme,
which you can read more about towards the end of this chapter, in
Section 8. So clearly I have a belief in the idea of leaving something
to settle before acting on it, or as we say, 'sleeping on it'. This is something I've often taught on my creative thinking courses, so you could
say that I have a core belief in this process. But this is not saying very
much, so I need to ask: 'What are the core beliefs that underlie this
notion?' Or to put it another way: 'Why is it that I think it's a valuable idea?' As I reflect on it I can see that it's partly because
of relevant experiences, such as the example of doing a cross-
word – get stuck, do something else, when you go back you see
the solution; and partly because I have a belief in the power of
the subconscious, so I believe that there is more to being human
than we recognize on the surface, that 'living in the now' is only
part of the story – while we consciously experience the world now,
there is part of us that works in the background (to use a computer
analogy), processing and relating ideas. A further belief that flows
from this is more contentious: it leads me to value uncertainty,
mystery and the aesthetic, which some might call spirituality: the

sense that there is more going on than meets the eye. So if I were to fill in such a table the first entry might look like this:

Thought	Core belief
If you walk away from something and forget about it for a while, you understand it better when you come back to it	Our subconscious works in the background, makes connections, sorts ideas and experience The here and now is only part of the story I value mystery and uncertainty

The process is one of making connections, of moving back step by step until you uncover the core beliefs behind your thoughts. So when you're ready, use the thoughts you put down in Exercise 2.8a to complete the following table:

Exercise 2.9a: Core beliefs – Written

Thought	Core belief

Completing these exercises should give you a set of core beliefs about yourself. For example:

- I believe that I'm no good at writing;
- I believe that I'm an interesting and engaging person;
- I believe that life has passed me by;
- I believe that we make our own luck;
- I believe that I'm a good homemaker;
- I believe that I don't make the most of my opportunities.

You'll see that this list has a mixture of practical beliefs, such as 'no good at writing' and 'good homemaker', and more general thoughts, such as 'life has passed me by' and 'interesting and engaging'. Your list might be very different, but hopefully it will contain the same sort of things to begin to work on.

Exercise 2.9b: Core beliefs – Thinking

Either:

1 Take one of the thoughts that you exposed in Exercise 2.8b.
2 Imagine how an actor might speak that thought out loud; think of them saying it on an open-air stage where in order for their voice to carry they must invest it with extra power and articulate it more fully; now see an intimate film version with an extreme close-up: What expression do they have? How is the scene shot to emphasize the thought and the 'thought behind the thought'? What kind of music is used in the scene?
3 Imagine that you are interviewing one of the actors and that they answer a question about their character by saying, 'Well you see, one of her/his core beliefs is ...'

Or:

1 Take one of the thoughts that you exposed in Exercise 2.8b.
2 Repeat it to yourself and then question it using the 'Why? Because ...' format.
  Example:
  Thought: 'They'll see through me.'
  Why?
  'Because I'm a charlatan.'

3 Formalize your answer into a core belief statement.
Example: 'I have a core belief that I'm a charlatan.'

Relating core beliefs to confidence situations

Exercise 2.10a: Core beliefs – Writing

1 Think of a situation in which you feel a lack of confidence. It could be anything – speaking to a large group, going into a room where people don't know you, speaking on the phone, meeting with a particular person, talking to your parents. Why do you find this difficult? Why does it drain your confidence? Now that you've had some practice using the Feelings–Thoughts–Core beliefs approach, apply it to your lack-of-confidence situation, asking yourself the following questions and writing down your own answers. Here's a worked example that might help give the idea.

Q What is the situation in which I feel a lack of confidence?
A Teaching a particular course.

Q How do you know that you are not confident in this situation?
A I don't look forward to it and I'd rather avoid it.

Q Can you describe the feelings?
A A sort of dread, not overpowering but destabilizing, uncomfortable.

Q What thoughts give rise to these feelings?
A Last time I taught this course it was a disaster. During the course the atmosphere was bad, I felt increasingly uncomfortable. Later, one member of the group complained to the course organizer and said that her view was shared by everyone there.

Q What core beliefs give rise to these thoughts?
A That when things go well, this is an aberration; at heart I believe I'm not very good at teaching and this group saw through me.

2 Now go through your answers again, this time with a decision to look critically but positively at the situation. Annotate what you've written, asking yourself new questions and adding new insights. Your aim is to give a fuller picture, one that enables you to be more balanced in your responses in such situations:

Q What is the situation in which I feel a lack of confidence?
A Teaching a particular course.

Notes: But I need to underline that it is this particular course. I feel more positive about other teaching I'm involved in, so there may be approaches I can transfer from other courses.

Q How do you know that you are not confident in this situation?
A I don't look forward to it and I'd rather avoid it.
Notes: But part of me also wants to 'embrace it', to do it and do it better – I think that this would 'take the curse off it'.

Q Can you describe the feelings?
A A sort of dread, not overpowering but destabilizing, uncomfortable.
Notes: I have to admit that this has become automatic now and that the feelings have a life of their own – they get exaggerated by being repeated so much.

Q What thoughts give rise to these feelings?
A Last time I taught this course it was a disaster. During the course the atmosphere was bad, I felt increasingly uncomfortable and one member of the group complained to the course organizer and said that her view was shared by everyone there.
Notes: But in fact only one person complained and she was clearly not engaging in the course while I was teaching it. I also have half a suspicion that she was on the wrong course but couldn't own up to it. There was also some positive feedback during the course and the feedback forms were reasonable, not nearly as negative as this one person's views.

Q What core beliefs give rise to these thoughts?
A That when things go well, this is an aberration; at heart I believe I'm not very good at teaching and this group saw through me.
Notes: And what about all the other courses I successfully teach? Do they back up this core belief?

3 Look over your notes and imagine that they have been written by someone else. It's a fact that we tend to judge ourselves far more harshly than we judge other people, so imagine that you are a supervisor, colleague, friend or professional counsellor of the person who's written the above; choose whoever fits the situation you've decided to explore. Write some supportive feedback for that person.

Exercise 2.10b: Core beliefs – Thinking

1 Read through your notes from Exercise 2.10a and identify a core belief of yours that affects your confidence.

2 Imagine the core belief engraved on a plaque in a public place. It looks solid and as if it will last for ever.

3 Imagine this scene: early one morning, when no one else is around, you approach the plaque with the core belief on it. At first you can't read it, but as you get nearer the familiar words gradually take focus. Then you begin to see something else: the plaque is covered with scratches – someone has scratched phrases into it, and every one starts with 'Yes, but ...' For example, on the plaque I see:

   'I find it difficult to talk to people in new situations.'

Scratched on it I see:

- Yes, but this is perfectly normal, most people are the same.
- Yes, but each one of your friends and colleagues was new to you at some point.
- Yes, but although you take time to get to know people, you do make new friends in time.
- Yes, but this is a problem you can overcome with a few simple strategies.
- Yes, but that's not always true, is it? What about that time when you...?

Finding solutions

The exercises so far have helped you to understand the core beliefs that might drain your confidence, and the last set of exercises should have thrown up some arguments to counteract those debilitating beliefs. But how can you put these thoughts to good, practical use when the chips are down and your unconfident feelings are holding hands with your unconfident thoughts and merrily bouncing up and down to the rhythm of your unconfident core beliefs?

Five practical suggestions

1 Knowledge is power Understanding a thing helps to rob it of its power to hurt us. Just knowing that your feelings are connected to your thoughts and your thoughts to your core beliefs gives you power over each. You are not suffering blindly, unable to work out what is going on; you are able to step back, analyse and form strategies.

If you find that you're simply overwhelmed by feelings of lack of confidence, repeat the exercises in this section until you are sure that you understand what's going on.

The very act of being able to step back and see the bigger picture takes you outside the maelstrom of your feelings; being able to see more clearly enables you to think more clearly and detach from your feelings of self-doubt.

2 Work on your core beliefs Do this as suggested in this section, and write down a list of positive beliefs to carry around with you, perhaps on a credit-card-sized card – three is a good number. This might seem like a simple exercise but its power lies in the work that has gone before. Do the exercises thoroughly so that what's on your card means something to you and is not just empty words.

Example core beliefs

I believe that it takes time for me to get to know new people – and this is okay.
I believe that other people are nervous in social situations.
I believe that I can help and support others, that there is a place for quieter, more reflective people in these situations.

Take a look at the card in private before you go into a situation in which you feel unconfident.

3 Recognize that we can change our beliefs about ourselves
Work on your core beliefs over time and feed in the positive experiences that you have along the way. By doing this you can transform negative and debilitating beliefs into positive and helpful ones. Taking the example above, we've come to see that 'I find it difficult to talk to people in new situations' is not the devastating negative idea that we once thought it was. It's perfectly fine to realize that some people find it difficult to talk to others in new situations and that this enables us to empathize with others in the same place. Over time – and it does take commitment – we can transform our negative core beliefs, so that although we acknowledge any truths they do contain, they no longer have the power to adversely affect our thoughts and our feelings.

4 Replace negative pictures What do you see in your mind when you think about your unconfident behaviour? Do you think of a specific instance, perhaps failing to be picked for a sports team or stumbling over your words in a presentation? Perhaps you have a more general image of an unconfident person and you see yourself in a negative light. For this exercise you need an image from memory, so find something and think of it as a photograph or as a freeze-frame in a film. Look at that image in your mind and then destroy it – utterly. You can have some fun with this: see it burn to ashes and watch the ashes blow away; see it melt to a blob, which gets eaten by a dog that then skips away into the distance; see it fold in and in on itself until it's a tiny dot that then disappears up its own fundament! Enjoy seeing the negative picture go, and make sure that it's really gone, blown away, melted, or burnt to nothing. Once it's gone you have a nice clear gallery space in your mind on which to hang a new picture, a positive picture. What will it be? An applauding crowd at the end of your speech? You sitting at your desk with a smile of satisfaction on your face? Or you opening a letter from your publisher enclosing a huge royalty cheque (guess where that came from)?

Use this visualization technique to undermine those negative feelings, thoughts and core beliefs, replacing them with positive versions. It really does make a difference once you realize that you have control over how you think.

5 Give the voices in your head the same treatment Perhaps you hear a voice saying, 'You're no good at interviews' or 'No one will want to talk to you.' We're going to think about getting rid of those voices by seeing them for the ridiculous, untrue, exaggerated things they are. Hear the voices in your head but get them to speak in a ridiculous fashion, so they sound like a Dalek or an over-the-top monster, or fast and squeaky like a Minnie Mouse cartoon character. Use your imagination: you're after anything that ridicules these voices, so keep repeating them until you're convinced that they sound completely dumb. Have a good laugh at them, then close the door firmly on them and never listen to them again. Should they ever dare to reappear in your mind, immediately put them into their funny mode, enjoy them for a bit and then banish them!

In conclusion

As you begin to recognize this Feelings–Thoughts–Core beliefs process, you'll probably find that you can work with it quickly as it arises, without going through the kind of meditative and reflective exercises in this section. With practice you can train yourself to respond to your feelings and see where they're coming from. You can learn to identify your core beliefs and see any truths they may contain in context. Over time – and once again, it does take commitment – we can transform our negative core beliefs so that, although we acknowledge any truths they contain, they no longer have the power to affect adversely our thoughts and our feelings.

5 Visualization, memory and imagination

In this section I want to look at some simple techniques that can help us overcome the feelings that lead to unconfident behaviour. As with everything in this book, you can take these ideas and adapt them to your personal circumstances and to what you find works for you, but all of them benefit from some sort of relaxation technique to help you to move away from negative feelings and to create the right environment for getting the most out of visualization. Have a go at some of the ideas in the section on relaxation (pp. 14–17), and then you're ready to try out some of these visualization techniques.

Replacing bad feelings with good memories

One of the simplest and most widespread visualization techniques is the use of imagination and memory to shift your thinking, and thus your feelings, from negative to positive. Let's take an example, one very familiar to many people: a visit to the dentist. Dentistry has a bad name, and in my case I remember some childhood horrors and an adult visit to a new dentist whose breath was more like whisky vapour at eleven in the morning (my confident behaviour in that case was to get out of his practice and never go back). However unfair this is to modern dentists, I am a coward when it comes to my yearly visits, and a complete jelly when treatment is required. My tone probably suggests that this is all a bit of a joke, and it's true that I do go for my check-ups and I do have the treatment, so I'm not as debilitated by it as I know some people are, and I've definitely improved over the years (thanks to my hero – see below). But I do sometimes get the old feeling of dread, particularly if a filling drops out or I break a tooth, so it is a real issue. You might be the same about dentists or it might be some other concern that has this power of bad feelings over you; the important thing is that memory, imagination and visualization can come to our aid. In my case, I'm very fortunate. For the past ten years or so I've had a wonderful dentist, Mr Rawal of St Albans. The man is a genius, with the very best of chair-side manners, and in all the years that I've been with him I've never had the slightest twinge of the discomfort and pain that I so fear from those childhood experiences. In fact when we moved south of London I stuck with him, so I now have a train journey of about one and a half hours to visit the dentist. I know it's mad but it works for me. So I have a model of a better experience to think about when that now irrational fear overtakes me. The technique is simplicity itself: when you feel that you're about to be assaulted by bad feelings, call to mind a time when things have gone well in a similar situation. All I have to do is focus on my last visit to the dentist and remember how well it went, and try to conjure up the wonderful feeling when it's all over and I didn't feel a thing. That little thought will still try to worm its way in: 'That was last time, but this time ...' But if you can detach the thought from the feelings that accompany it by the power of memory and visualization, then you can deal with the thought rationally: 'All my experience tells me that things will be okay again this time; there's no reason to believe that they won't.'

A refinement of this technique, which many find useful, is to use a physical trigger to help you summon up the positive feeling. It works like this: visualize the positive – the last pain-free trip to the dentist, the last successful presentation, or the time you chatted away happily at that party once you'd met the right person. With the visualization will come the positive, calm feelings. Once you're in that constructive frame of mind, perform a simple physical action, such as pressing a finger into your palm or squeezing your ear lobe. Repeat the thought and action a few times and before long you'll be able to summon the positivity just by doing the action. The theory is that the feeling will have become attached to the act. Try this out for yourself. I have to say that it's not a technique that helps me, because I find the imagination is enough without the physical trigger. But since we're all different it may well work for you.

Exercise 2.11

What are the situations that press the anxiety button for you and bring on unconfident feelings? You could use the following table to add focus to your thinking. There are some examples followed by space for your own concerns.

Situation	What I feel anxious about	Useful memory
A visit to the dentist	It will hurt like it did when I was a child	Last time I went, and the time before, and the time before…
Taking something back to a shop for a refund	The shop assistant will be unhelpful and rude; I'll end up feeling embarrassed	I asked at the time of purchase if it would be possible to return the item. I've returned things before to this shop with no problems
A job interview	I'll get tongue-tied, forget what I want to say and make a fool of myself	I did okay on my interview a while back

What if you have nothing to put in the last column of Exercise 2.11? There are occasions when we face something that makes us anxious and we don't have previous good experiences to visualize, so in that situation is everything lost? Here are a couple of visualization, memory and imagination techniques that can come to our aid.

Understanding

The first is hardly a technique at all; it's just the simple process of understanding your fear. One valuable approach is to understand the link between feelings, thoughts and core beliefs, as explored in Section 4. Once we understand where our feelings are coming from, we begin to manage them and they can no longer overwhelm us. They might still be troublesome and need further work, but we are back in the driving seat and are no longer panicked into inaction by overbearing feelings heading towards us in an unstoppable rush.

Go somewhere that's good for you

This is the well-known technique of having a secret place that you can imagine yourself in, a place with memories of peacefulness and calm, of wholeness and positivity, the kind of place where just being there gives you a feeling of being at one with yourself, quietly confident and tranquil. For many people this is a real place, perhaps somewhere you've been on holiday; for others it's imaginary, perhaps a composite of real places you know. In order to put yourself there, and get the benefit of the accompanying feelings, use the relaxation techniques in Section 1 and then simply dwell in, and focus on, this special place, enjoying its qualities and positive atmosphere. Use this both to separate yourself from the anxious feelings and to gain perspective so that you can see the feelings for what they are and recognize that they are not as big and overpowering as you thought.

If you find that your anxieties intrude on your special place, take the time to step back and gain fresh perspective, take your deep breaths again and then re-enter your special place in your imagination with a renewed sense of joy at being there.

One final thought on this kind of visualization: some people find it helpful to have an object or a picture to use as a focus, to help them to transport themselves to the special place. My wife is quite lucky in this regard as one of her special places is Macarellata Beach in Menorca (the one that you can walk to from Macarella), and this is so beautiful that it is featured on many postcards, advertisements and posters – so it is easy to carry an image around. In my book *The Creative Path: Living a More Vibrant Life* (Azure, 2004) I wrote about an image that does the same thing for me:

> On my office wall I have a photograph of a bluebell wood that I took at a time when I was facing big decisions that I didn't feel equipped to take. It's quite a good photo but it's not anything particularly original and it doesn't offer much in the way of insight to anyone except me. For me it symbolizes a moment when I was reaching forward, wanting to be different, to make changes; and the mind picture that I used of that 'good future' was of standing in the midst of those bluebells – again not an original or clever idea, just something that worked for me at that time. Now I'm living in that future, and I use the picture as a reminder of the steps that I took: how I was then and how I am now.

Your trigger or ticket into your special place may be an image or it may be an object like a pebble or shell or something that means something only to you. Whatever it is, or whether you don't use any kind of physical symbol, try to get into the habit of being able to go to your special place in your mind whenever you need to. As with all things, this kind of visualizing improves with practice, so try it out whenever you can so that it's available to you when you really need it to help you overcome feelings of inadequacy and lack of confidence. In time you can add more places to meet a range of different situations:

When I'm feeling ...	I imagine ...
Restless, can't sleep, agitated	Macarellata Beach
Uncertain about the future	Bluebell wood
I can't do this	In the green room surrounded by family and friends offering congratulations

Where do you feel it?

This is a simple imaginative technique that, like so many of the ideas in the book, begins with stepping back, gaining perspective and not allowing yourself to simply be swept along by your feelings without let or hindrance.

You're about to do something that you find difficult and you're not feeling very confident about it:

- pause;
- step back;
- think about what you are feeling;
- ask yourself where that feeling seems to be located in your body.

This may seem a strange thing to do if you've never done it before, but if you think about it, we often relate feelings to body locations: I had butterflies in my stomach; my feet were rooted to the spot; my head was buzzing; my heart leapt into my mouth – these are all phrases we might use about or relate to feelings. So it is not so strange to realize that our feelings often seem to reside somewhere inside us. But another reason that we might find this difficult to grasp is that as a society we have a few hundred years behind us of thinking that our bodies carry our brains, which generate our consciousness. This is true, but it can lead us to think of our thoughts and feelings as separate from our bodies, which are mere conveyances; in fact body, mind and consciousness are more intimately linked than this, and body image and the location of our bodies in space are part of our overall consciousness. There are 100 million nerve endings in the gut, and although these are mainly concerned with subconscious actions such as moving food along, they also affect us consciously through feelings of hunger and satiety, for example. So the mind, through the nervous system, is integrated with the body. In some senses we think with our bodies – do you pace to and fro when thinking something through? Perhaps you bury your head in your hands to shut out the world when you need to concentrate? Ever punched the air with joy at a goal achieved or some very good news? You'll find more on this in Section 2 on body language of course, but here let's take forward the idea of our feelings being located in our bodies. Here's where a course participant located his anxious feelings:

Feeling	Location
Too much change, too fast and I can't cope with it	Stomach tight and tense
I'm worried about something and can't see the way forward	Shoulders tense
I'm not sure I'm going to be appreciated at this event	Tightness in the throat
I'm nervous, keyed up (such as before a big event)	Stomach and lungs – breathing is shallow

Have a go for yourself. This can take time and practice if you're not used to thinking in this way, but many people find that once they start searching for the locations of their feelings, they click into the process quickly and easily.

Working on those locations

For many people, identifying the location is the key to dealing with the feeling effectively because once you realize where you feel what you feel, you can learn to relax that area either through massage or simple breathing and relaxing exercises, for example:

Location	Relaxation technique
Stomach tight and tense	Consciously relax, take deep breaths, imagine your stomach uncoiling and relaxing. There are also yoga and other massage techniques that can help unknot a knotted stomach
Shoulders tense	Deep breathing, massage
Tightness in the throat	Deep breathing, gently massage with one hand
Stomach and lungs – breathing is shallow	Consciously relax, deep breathing

You can use the relaxation techniques in Section 1 to put yourself in the right frame of mind for any of the above. Yoga and other relaxation and exercise techniques are beyond the scope of this book but are well worth investigating and can powerfully support these visualization approaches.

If you find that identifying the location and relaxation don't take you far enough in allaying the negative feelings, you can try the following technique – but it does come with a 'health warning', although it's not dangerous (except perhaps to your public image). It comes under the category of what one of my freelance training colleagues at the BBC describes as 'somewhat Californian', meaning a bit out of the mainstream and tending towards the wacky – so approach with care, especially if you're British!

You've located the feeling in a part of your body; let's say it's in your stomach. Picture it there, perhaps as a cloud of distress or as a gelatinous mass of some sort. Then imagine that you are pulling the feeling out. Put your hand on the area where you feel the negativity and pull it away from your body. Imagine every last bit of the feeling coming away and then flick it off your hand and away into the air where it disappears. The feeling's gone.

Does it work?

I think so. It seems to work for me as a short-term fix. I've seen hypnotherapists do a similar thing with specific anxieties, where the therapist will suddenly reach towards you and mime plucking the feeling away. Some claim that this can permanently remove negativity. I've no idea if this is so but I do think that the power of our imagination is extraordinary and that often we don't appreciate this.

There's a parallel with folk remedies, such as those for warts that involve rubbing an old bone on the wart and then throwing it over your shoulder; or tying some thread over the wart, then burying the thread – by the time it's rotted, the wart is gone. It seems that, like placebos in medical trials, these 'imaginary' approaches often do the trick. I had a persistent verruca for about five years and tried everything the chemist could sell. Then I decided to try visualization techniques and in a month it was gone. This is not scientifically valid, of course, as there was no control, and who knows whether it might have gone if I'd done nothing; whether it was just its time to go. So I am not suggesting that we can simply think ourselves well, but visualizing the removal of negative feelings is certainly worth a go – it might work for you when dealing with feelings that inhibit and restrict your confidence.

Look up

> 'I will lift up mine eyes unto the hills, from whence cometh my help.'
>
> (Psalm 121, King James Version)

Another simple technique for dealing with negative feelings is to look up. If you've not heard of this, you might want to read that sentence again because that's really all there is to it. The suggestion is, and again I find this to be true, that if you look up above the horizon you cannot connect with your negative feelings. You can still think the thoughts but you can't feel the feelings. When I first heard this, and it was the aforementioned BBC colleague who told me (so who's sounding Californian now!), it sounded like a cure-all for the world's problems: look up, world leaders, and war will be no more; look up, angry teenager, and feel bright and positive; look up and there will never be an unconfident person in this world. I quickly realized that you simply can't live your life looking up all the time: I tried it walking along a busy shopping street in Belfast and narrowly avoided finding myself looking up from a prone position on the pavement. But you can use it to break out of a cycle of negative thoughts and thus give yourself a better chance of being confident. You can use it at the start of other techniques to avoid starting off with bad feelings about yourself.

Does it work?

Some people I've suggested this to have not found it helpful, but many do – try it and see. I find that it works best when your eyes look up well above the horizon rather than just moving your head – if you think about it this must be so, otherwise the notion of lying in bed staring at the ceiling would not work as an image of ennui and depression.

Why does it work?

I don't know, but one possibility is that our evolution has trained us to be on the lookout for danger, to scan the horizon; and that when we do this we are not to be distracted but are to be focused and alert, so everything else drops away except the task in hand.

Another way of looking at this is to return to the notion of how we use our bodies (see Section 2, 'Body language'); in this instance, adopting an outward-looking positive stance creates the appropriate feelings within us.

6 Learning your stuff!

The best way to inspire confidence in yourself and others is to know what you're talking about so well and in such depth that you can respond easily and with flair to whatever you're asked. Let's be realistic: there are times when you simply have to learn some facts and figures, a speech or a presentation, which you'll deliver using notes or even learnt by heart. For some people this is very scary. Others, however daunting they find it, only feel comfortable if they have learnt 'their words' or at least their opening, to help them get over their initial nervousness.

If I have to give any sort of presentation, I use a simple set of notes with key points and bulleted sub-headings, and I speak to these without further written material apart from handouts to give to the delegates (and they can be a useful memory jogger in themselves). Others use a similar approach but with small 'cue cards', usually index cards, that can be easily held in the palm of the hand and turned over as needed. This looks neater and has the advantage of breaking down what you want to say into bite- or card-sized chunks. For me there'd always be the fear of getting them out of order, and using stapled sheets or sheets in a folder avoids this complication.

Where I come unstuck, if I'm not careful and rigorous in my preparation, is on those occasions where I have to learn something by heart. In my case this is usually lines for an acting audition or performance, so I'm going to share here some of the tips I've learnt and developed over the years.

Allow time

Give yourself the time you need to practise, building in plenty of learning time. You can make the most of the time you have by finding odd moments to go through your words: when you have five minutes to sit down, in your lunch break, in the bath (print off several copies to allow for steam degeneration), on a train journey and so on. The prime time is just before you go to sleep, so have a look at a short section when you go to bed as it really is true that the things we read before sleep stick with us. I often find that I struggle through trying to remember something at night but I'm word-perfect in the morning – it's equally true that about half of it has leaked out of the brain by lunchtime, but that's another story.

Stick a copy to the fridge or somewhere equally convenient (for a long speech do this section by section) so that when cooking, ironing or bathing the gerbil you can sneak a quick glance and practise as you work. As you get to know the piece you can go over it any time – when walking, for example. I find swimming is terrific for line-learning as the rhythm of going up and down the pool with regular strokes aids the learning process. Perhaps, though, all my acting comes out sounding like the speaking clock with evenly spaced pauses...

Understand

It's true of acting and it's true of any kind of presentation, that unless you understand what you're saying you can't deliver it with conviction. Go through what you have to say and, if you're allowed to, edit it so that it is in the kind of language that you would naturally use when speaking, and so that you're completely comfortable with the words and their meaning. There is clearly a difference between written and spoken English, so that brings us right on to the next point.

Practise out loud

Until you speak the words aloud, you won't know what works and what doesn't. You don't have to give full projection to your voice when practising, although it's a good idea to have at least a couple of runs at full volume and as much like 'for real' as possible. People walking past our house recently might well have heard me shouting at the top of my voice, 'You Jade, you slut. The devil take her the wretched creature', as I rehearsed a piece of Molière for an audition. They may have thought I like shouting at my wife, but I hope they appreciated the quality of the insults!

Get an audience

Find someone you trust and, when you're ready, go through your speech or presentation for them, asking them to tell you if you drop your voice, if any parts are unclear or could be phrased better and so on. Also ask them to take account of body language (see Section 2 above).

Picture and wordplay

I try to learn an acting part from the character outwards: I think about who I'm meant to be, and try to understand the thought processes that lead the character to say what he says in the order in which he says it. You can apply the same principle to any speech or presentation, except that the character isn't Dracula or Argon the hypochondriac, but 'the person who knows about *x*' or 'the one who's going to clearly explain *y*' – you may not be playing a character but you'll certainly be playing a role. This 'from the inside' approach is fine for many speeches but it doesn't always help. For example, in *The Hypochondriac*, the Molière play I mentioned above, Argon goes through various lists of treatments he's had. He obviously loves his medicines and 'injections' but there is no logical reason why 'a small injection, preparatory, insinuative and emollient' should come before 'a sound purgative and stimulating concoction', yet I have to learn them in the right order so I use a couple of tricks that you might find helpful. For the first, I thought about a pie, because it's a strong and surprising visual image in the context (so I'm more likely to remember it), and it gave me the initial letters of 'preparatory, insinuative and emollient'. So when learning this piece for the first time I trained myself to think 'pie' and that image popped up as I approached the line, which helped me to remember the words and their order. Later, I was having trouble with 'a sound purgative and stimulating concoction', so I put the image of a radio in my mind to remind me of sound. I found that, over time, once I got to the radio, then to sound, the rest came along with it.

These visual and wordplay tricks can help in the initial stages, then as meaning and rote-learning take over, they fade away, their job done. Your job, however, is to keep practising and practising again, wherever and whenever you can, as this is the only sure way of getting those words to stick.

My final pieces of advice are: not to go on learning right up to the last minute – it's more important to arrive relaxed and full of energy at the start of your speech or presentation; and if you can, take some notes or cue cards with you – you probably won't need them, but in part this will be because you know they're there.

7 Small talk

By 'small talk' I mean casual social interaction, often between strangers or people you know slightly or people you know in a different context. For example, you might be very comfortable speaking with someone at work but find it difficult to know what to say if you find yourself standing next to him or her at the office party. Or you might arrive for a meeting early and have two or three people to chat with and not have a clue what to say to them. I've given this a section of its own because it has often come up during workshops and coaching; it's clearly something that a lot of people find problematic. I'm certainly not immune to this, as I hope the following story illustrates.

A tale of two parties

A few years back I did a couple of days' work for a BBC department that I hadn't worked with before. Six months or so later they very kindly invited me to their Christmas party. Of course I accepted; no freelancer ever passes up the opportunity for a bit of festive networking. Okay, I also couldn't resist the free drink, food and revelry. Food and drink there were but not much revelry, at least not for me. I arrived at the noisy West End wine bar and realized that I didn't really know anyone. I couldn't remember the names of the people I'd worked with six months earlier and it was soon pretty clear that no one really knew who I was or why I was there. I stood around for a bit with a drink in my hand; I went to the loo, stood around some more, and drank some more. I tried a bit of small talk but it was difficult in the noisy atmosphere and I began increasingly to focus on what I was doing – not fitting in. I became acutely aware of how I was standing, how many sips of wine I was taking and so on. Eventually I did get chatting to someone but pretty soon disaster struck when it dawned on us both that she wasn't who I thought she was (she looked blank when I mentioned working together a few years back), and I had never in fact seen her before! Thankfully the cabaret started at this point and I was able to stand with the crowd and laugh a bit before slipping quietly away.

A couple of years later I did a little bit more work for the same department and again they kindly invited me to their party and again I accepted. This time the wine bar was quieter. There were a couple of entertainers on hand, so there was always something to watch – a table magician and a caricature artist. I fell in with the artist, and my portrait was sketched fairly early on. Armed with this masterpiece I found that I had something to talk about. I developed a line, 'Looks like Shakespeare, don't you think?' It didn't – much – but that was fine because people could then say, 'No, more like Ken Dodd – but nothing like you, of course' or whatever. In other words, we had something to talk about. I found a table and sat down with a drink, did my caricature spiel and then got chatting to someone I'll call Pam (her real name was Pamela) who turned out, in an almost exact reversal of the previous fiasco, to be someone I had vaguely known years ago. She knew of me and introduced me in glowing terms (we'd all had a few drinks by then) to her mates. Dancing, more magic and fun ensued, and Pam and I were married three weeks later.

Okay, I made up that last bit, but the rest is true and you may well be thinking how feeble I am not even to be able to chat to people at a Christmas party. But as I said, many people find this kind of thing difficult, and although I'm usually fine in this sort of situation, in the first case I wasn't. So what lessons can we learn from these party stories?

Be prepared

I went to the first party without a thought about who would be there; it would have been so easy to have looked up the names of the people I'd worked with that year. I could even have emailed one or two to ask them what they were up to and to say that I'd see them at the party. I could also, as this was a media do, have looked up some of the department's recent output and noted who had made it, so that I would at least have had a starting point for conversation. I did this in readiness for the second party but, as you've read, this time they'd put in the preparation, and the magician and artist provided the way in.

Take the focus off yourself

That caricature was a godsend. I could talk about it and not about me. Assuming that you're not going to have that sort of gift, think about what you could take as a conversation starter.

This will depend on the type of event and who will be there, but it can be anything, such as, 'I saw these postcards in a shop on the way here. They're unusual, don't you think?'

There doesn't have to be a physical focus for this approach. Find out a bit about the building you're in if this is likely to be a point of interest, or the town. You're just looking for something to get you launched into a conversation – so we're really back to preparation again.

Why be afraid of silence?

There's that awful feeling when we're so alertly aware, thinking that we should fill a silence but don't know what to say. Why do we so hate silence? One reason could be a concern about what others think of us, so we set up a vicious circle of 'She thinks I'm being impolite or boring so I must say something, but I don't know what to say, so she thinks I'm being impolite or boring...'

I believe that we should try to become more comfortable with silence in social situations, but I accept that many of us fear that it might be taken for rudeness; so a few well-chosen words can help to ease the situation:

'I'm just going to sit for a moment and catch my breath.'

'I'm going to read through my notes for a few moments before we get started.'

'I must just jot down a few thoughts before the meeting, if you'll excuse me.'

8 Creativity and confidence: the Quintessence method

To finish this round-up of confidence-boosting tools I'm going to explore the cryptically named Quintessence method. Let's start with that name: it's called 'Quintessence – the five-pointed star of creative change' because it's a five-point plan and, er, that's it – except that I thought it sounded good and would create the necessary intrigue factor when it appeared on course materials and in articles and books (see Figure 2.1). You might think otherwise!

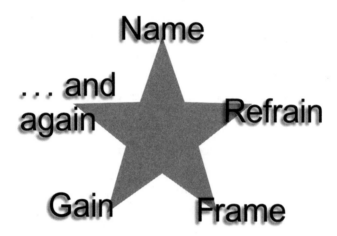

Figure 2.1 Quintessence: the five-pointed star of creative change
Copyright © Gordon Lamont 2004

The basic idea is that you begin at the top with 'Name' and work clockwise around the star until you get to '… and again', and after an appropriate time you can go back to 'Name' and start all over again. It's a creative thinking method that's intended to help you find new ways forward when you're stuck in a rut, and so is ideal for applying to confidence issues. I've used this on confidence courses and it's a powerful way of coming up with fresh thinking and new things to try. Here's what each of the points of the star is about:

Name

This simply means naming your issue, getting something clear and unambiguous that you want to work on. Try to be as focused and precise as you can. For example, 'I want to be more confident about speaking in meetings' rather than 'I want to be more confident.' It's good to set and focus on specific goals, otherwise we can let our negative core beliefs run riot – they just love an unstructured vacuum.

At a recent confidence course for The Talk Consultancy <www.talkconsultancy.com> I demonstrated the method by taking an idea thrown up by the delegates. They chose to work on 'How can I take criticism better?' and used the method to good effect, so we'll take that as our example.

Having named the issue in a precise way, write it down so that you can use the method over a number of days, returning to it whenever you have time. Writing an idea down also helps to firm it up. The very process of choosing, refining and naming the issue begins the creative thinking process, so go with the flow and throw the idea around in your mind, beginning to understand and explore it. You're ready now to move on to the next point of the star.

Refrain

Not a chorus in this case but a step back, a letting-go for a while. Once you've clearly named and acknowledged the issue you want to work on, there will come a point when you start to notice that you're not getting anywhere with it; the same thoughts go round and round, and that's the time to put the issue aside, sleep on it or go and do something else. I wrote earlier about how this works for crosswords or other puzzles, and it's just the same for imaginative thinking – leave it alone for a bit, and when you come back to it you'll be refreshed and will see new possibilities.

Frame

In many ways this is the heart of the method and it's all about seeing the issue in a different way; seeing it as if through a frame. A frame can be anything – here are some examples:

Film camera	See the issue in close-up or from a high angle, for example.
Dream	Imagine that you dreamt about the issue. What symbols would appear and what would the story be?
Someone else's shoes	Imagine that you are someone else in the scenario you're thinking about. How do they see it? What do they think and feel?
On a screen	An approach with Buddhist overtones: imagine that you are detached, seeing the scenario play out on a screen – you're not involved, you observe and reflect.
If it were a...	This is the well-known game of 'If he were a car he'd be a ...' 'If this situation were a film it would be a comedy/war movie/shocker etc.'

There are many 'framed' ways of thinking about an issue. They are all about seeing it differently and finding some new understanding. Take our example of 'How can I take criticism better?' Using the frame of a film camera, think about someone criticizing you and see it from a wide high-angle shot, which would literally help you to get perspective as you realize how small this incident is and how much other important stuff is going on around you. Alternatively, you might replay what was said in slow motion so that you can concentrate on everything that you heard – not just what you thought you heard. Combine this with an 'on a screen' frame and you might be able to see the situation more objectively.

I'll give an example of a 'dream' frame, starting with a story well known in dream literature, namely that of Elias Howe, co-inventor of the sewing machine. Here's a version of his famous dream, with a health warning about his unenlightened view about indigenous peoples!

> Elias has been working hard all day because he knows that there's a lot of money to be made from the first practical sewing machine, but he can't get it right – either the material snags or

the needles snap. Exhausted, he finally gives in for the night and goes to bed, but his mind is still working on the problem and, in his dreams, his subconscious speaks to him...

In the dream he is running for his life. A gang of 'cannibals' is chasing him and he can't escape [this is the 1840s, so 'cannibals' are very much in the air]. He runs, but knows that it's hopeless; he is both running and not running – a common dream experience.

The next moment, in the way that dreams shift scene so fluidly, he is in the cooking pot, in very hot water (a resonant phrase for anyone with difficulties; and dreams are not averse to using pictograms and puns to speak to us).

He climbs out of the pot but the 'cannibals', moving as one, lean over, and their pointed wooden spears push him back in with a jabbing action. Again he tries to climb out and again he is pushed back – their spears pushing down then pulling back ... Desperate now, he attempts to climb out one more time; again the spears push, jab and withdraw...

It's too much; he wakes up; it's over; his heart is racing; but he says again and again to himself, 'It was a dream, Elias, it was a dream.' The fear is mixed with a joyous relief, an escape – thank God. And then, hot and wet from the horrors of the cooking pot, it strikes him: the spears strike him, but what a happy attack this is – a sharp pointed, acute and undeniable moment of realization. He sees the spears afresh and realizes that their movement is like the needle of his prototype sewing machine, jabbing down and up; but he also sees an important detail: every spear has a hole in the sharp end. It's the breakthrough he's been looking for.

All previous attempts at making a sewing machine had been based on a needle like that used for hand sewing, with the eye at the opposite end to the point. Howe now realized that he could devise a mechanism that would allow the thread to be poked through the material by a needle with an eye at the sharp end, and then be anchored by thread from underneath – and so the sewing machine was born.

(The Elias Howe dream story is told in *A Popular History of American Invention*, edited by Waldemar Kaempffert, Vol. II (C. Scribner's Sons, 1924) and in many a book on dreams since then.)

There are plenty of stories of people making breakthroughs as their subconscious speaks to them through dreams, but the important point in using dreams as thinking frames is to concentrate on how they get to the essence of an issue by using metaphors, symbols, wordplay (like 'hot water') and puns. So you ask yourself, 'If I had a dream about this situation, what might it be?'

One of the many ideas that came up on the course I mentioned was that if you dreamt about 'How can I take criticism better?' the dream might go something like this:

'I'm floating on a cloud having a relaxing drink. I look down and see people like ants going about their busy lives far below me.'

This is a dream about perspective and about dealing with the issue from a relaxed viewpoint rather than in the heat of the moment, and it is just one example among many framing possibilities. At the course it represented a breakthrough for at least one delegate, who was enabled to see some issues in a completely different light for the first time.

1 + 1 = New

One other type of framing is encapsulated in a phrase I use: '1 + 1 = New'. Yes, I know it's back to being 'Californian' but it does sum up the simple idea, and it is memorable. It works like this: take the issue and put it with something different to see what comes up. The human mind is brilliant at making connections. We see our lives as stories, connecting one part to another; we put random events together as we seek for and create meaning. So play 1 + 1 = New and see what fresh ideas emerge. One way to do this is to use a dictionary in a random fashion. I have a dictionary in front of me as I write, and I'm going to open it at random, point to a word without looking and then make a connection with our issue of 'How can I take criticism better?'

Okay, I've done that, and the word I landed on is 'Pierrot' – the character from French pantomime.

How can we relate this to the issue? This one's almost too easy: pantomime is an exaggerated theatre form, so you could use the image of Pierrot as a reminder of how you exaggerate what you think people are saying; how you respond in an over-the-top way. In your mind, let Pierrot respond to the criticism with larger-than-life hurt – big movements and unsubtle blown-up facial responses; let this image speak to you of how your responses can be over-the-top.

Just to prove the technique, here's another genuinely random word: shelf life. Another easy one: most criticisms fade over time; either we learn to accept the small truth they might contain and thus they lose their sting, or we lose interest in them or simply forget them as we move on, change and develop. So we can see a criticism in perspective and realize that it too will have a shelf life after which it will be gone.

One more: monochrome. I have some thoughts on this one, but why don't you have a go at connecting our example issue – or any other – to this word in a creative and constructive way?

Work with framing, trying a number of different approaches until you find something helpful, and then move on to the next point of the Quintessence star. If you find that you can't relax enough to do your creative thinking because the issue is too upsetting, go back to 'Refrain' and have some time off to allow your mind to process 'offline' for a bit before returning to 'Frame'.

Gain

This is a vital part of the process. All this creativity and confidence-building stuff is great but it's just a sticking plaster or a few moments of 'feelgood' unless it actually makes a real difference to you and how you live, what you think and feel and how you behave. It needs to make a difference, and this is the 'Gain' part of the process. Having worked with frames to find some deeper understanding, ask yourself: 'What am I going to do to turn that knowledge and perception into practical steps, real ways forward?'

The trick here is to allow yourself to think small: even simply writing down your first step might be a big first step in itself if it's an issue that you've avoided in the past; you're committing it to paper and so acknowledging its reality. Some other small but significant steps around confidence issues might be:

I want to phone Jill, who I think might be avoiding me.	I will write down some things to say so that I don't get flustered (ask her about her children, holiday etc.). I will put her number in my book so that I can take it with me for whenever I have a spare moment.
I want to send in my short story to a magazine.	I will ask three friends to read it. I will print off ten copies and ask if I can leave them in health centres, community centres etc. I will include a feedback form (set up a PO box or ask the surgery to collect them if you're concerned about leaving your contact details for strangers). I will explore writers' groups in the area.
I want to become better at putting my ideas across in meetings.	I will write key points on cards so that I can refer to them easily. I'll talk to a couple of people beforehand to see what they think about my ideas. I'll practise talking slowly and clearly and try to lower my voice to come over as more authoritative.

I want to stop feeling intimidated by the gang of youths outside.	I will write down why I feel intimidated – how much is to do with things that have actually happened and how much is to do with exaggerated fears that I dwell on unnecessarily? I will find out about community groups and community policing so that I can discuss and understand this issue more fully.
I want to get a better job.	I will make a list of reasons why I want to change jobs and be realistic about the advantages/disadvantages of my current job. I will try to be detached and investigate the possibilities with a clear vision of what's available and what might be appropriate to me. I will identify one possible job and try to find someone I can talk to about it.

The delegates at the confidence course came up with lots of practical ideas for how they could respond better to criticism, but they all began with the vital notion of gaining perspective as in the dream mentioned above. Perspective would enable them to:

• see the truth or otherwise in the criticism;
• react rationally without emotions clouding the issue;
• find positive responses to build on what was said;
• separate what was actually said from what was assumed or interpreted;
• understand how the reaction relates to core beliefs (see Section 4);
• plan a positive way forward.

The group recognized that these things were easy to say but hard to put into practice, so the Gain was to find a way of reminding themselves of the need for and value of perspective on a daily basis. One idea was to write their key messages about perspective on a small card like a 'pledge card' and carry this around with them. Another idea is to use a 'talisman', something that would act as a reminder – perhaps a pebble or shell that you keep on your desk or in your pocket. It doesn't have to symbolize anything by its form – you simply decide that this is your 'perspective shell' and whenever you see it or touch it, its job is to remind you of the importance of seeing things in perspective. In fact you can usually find a creative link between the object and its purpose (although it might be a tenuous one): a pebble offers the perspective of having been part of a very different world of time and geology; a shell carries the notion of protection and a safe place to retreat to.

... and again

Confidence work is never done. How could it be? Things change and develop; today's debilitating issue is superseded by the unexpected tomorrow; that big issue melts away and no longer demands your attention; or perhaps you even become *too* confident in one area and need to reflect on that!

The final part of the Quintessence approach is a reminder to revisit every so often, to reassess where you are and perhaps restart the whole process. To stick with our example, you may decide that having worked on it and made some progress you need to rename 'How can I take criticism better?' by calling it 'I can learn from criticism but how can I feed back my responses to unfair criticism?'

I hope you find something useful in the Quintessence method and the confidence toolkit as a whole. The emphasis has been on confidence as something you *do*, so it can involve hard work. But that makes the achievement all the sweeter and more valuable.

3

Sixty-three confidence boosters

Here are a few ideas to help when your confidence needs a boost. There are all sorts, from the entirely practical, such as 'Breathe' (4), to the more 'far out', such as 'Talk to your past self' (28). They won't all suit all readers, so take a look and see what works for you. A number of the ideas are snapshot versions of material in the eight sections of Chapter 2, 'Confidence toolkit', and in these cases you'll find cross-references back to that main material. Other ideas are self-explanatory and stand alone.

Why 63 ideas? Why not? I set out to write 50 but decided that I had a few more to add. I know books are supposed to be neat and tidy with lists of ten or 50 or 99 or 100. Let me confidently assert that I have 63.

1 Feel unconfident

This may seem a very strange way to begin a list of confidence boosters, but it's here, right at the top of the list, for a very good reason. Throughout this book we've focused on the idea that there are things we can do, actions we can undertake to change the situations, often those in our own heads, that lead to feelings of a lack of confidence. So the idea here is that if you choose to, and it is your choice, you can focus on feeling unconfident or you can identify an issue and find small positive steps that will take you forward. There are all the ideas below to read and consider – even if you reject all but one, that still gives you something to try. For a step by step process you might want to look at the Quintessence method in Section 8 of Chapter 2. So choose to feel unconfident or choose to ignore your feelings and address a particular situation.

2 Read a book

This is really two tips in one. Assuming, and it's a big assumption, that you've read all or much of this book, flick through it with a determination to take one of the ideas in here and make it your own – shape and adapt it to your situation and try something out. Or, of course, you can do the same with another book addressing confidence issues.

The other way that reading a book can help with confidence is the wonderful power of literature – by which I mean any writing, fact or fiction, that works for you – to take us 'out of ourselves', to give us a fresh perspective and a window on the lives and into the souls of others. Anything that takes the focus away from a negative introspection is good for us, helping us to see the bigger picture and putting our concerns into a helpful context.

3 Do something naughty but nice

Give yourself a guilt-free treat every so often. There's a huge difference between 'doing what we ought to do' because of a fear of the disapproval of others, and doing what we want to do because we've made a rational decision about it. Diet very obviously comes to mind as something that our society is concerned about for good health reasons and, perhaps, for not so good body-image reasons. The 'naughty' part of this is about making a decision to ignore those disapproving (though often imaginary) looks and comments and to have the confidence to 'do it my way' – whatever it is!

4 Breathe

A good idea in general!

To calm yourself and help you focus, take a few moments to breathe deeply. Adopt a relaxed posture and breathe in slowly; you're aiming to take the breath from your diaphragm and not to breathe shallowly from the top of your lungs. Imagine that as you breathe in through your nose you are smelling your favourite wine, and as you breathe out you are gently causing a candle flame to flicker.

There's lots more on relaxation and breathing in Section 1 of Chapter 2.

5 Still yourself

Develop a relaxation method that suits you and your circumstances. We don't all have the time and space to do a yoga session or even watch a yoga video in our own home. If you do, make this or other relaxation techniques part of your routine; but if you don't, work out what you can do, perhaps on public transport or by getting up ten minutes earlier. Your routine should include breathing exercises, muscle tensing and relaxing and perhaps some form of visualization, as explored in Section 4 of Chapter 2. If you're a desk-based worker, you can develop a simple routine at your desk. There's more on relaxation and breathing in Section 1 of Chapter 2.

6 Meditate

Once you're in your relaxed state, what are you going to do there? You could try some simple meditation related to confidence, such as the next four ideas, numbers 7 to 10, on the following pages. Or you could try this: think about the pictures and photographs that you have around you at home or at work or in your wallet. Choose one that you particularly like and meditate on its qualities. Why does it speak to you? Why does it make you 'feel good'? If it had a voice, what would it say to you? Can you take its 'message', its positive essence, and use this to boost your confidence?

There's more on meditation and visualization in Section 5 of Chapter 2.

7 Replace bad feelings with good memories

Don't let the negative rule; find good positive memories to counteract the bad and negative, and have them always available to draw on when needed. We all have a tendency to give the negative more credence than it deserves; two people praised your last piece of work but included some suggestions for changes. Do you concentrate more on the suggestions, subtly changing them from suggestions to criticisms and then to complaints? Keep the positive comments in mind too and work on getting a balanced memory of the event. This is even more important when dealing with long-established memories that we have encrusted over the years with an undue negativity. Take them out and give them a clean-up with the magic ingredient 'balance' – don't just accept what they've become. See Section 4 of Chapter 2.

8 Get perspective on those negative voices

You don't have to listen to the incessant chatter in your head that tells you you're no good at this or that, or that this will happen because it always does. Hear these voices for what they are, expose them by examining what they seem to be saying in the balanced light of experience. See Section 4 of Chapter 2.

9 Ridicule those negative voices

Hear them in your head as funny, cartoon-like and silly! Negative voices can have a nagging quality, so start with that thought and exaggerate it until they become the voices of silly nagging characters – airheads who wouldn't understand a balanced picture if it was of scales on a tightrope. Then have fun playing with them in an audio fashion; go mad with robot voices and daft superhero types. Once you hear them for what they are, they're no longer powerful. See Section 4 of Chapter 2.

10 Replace negative pictures

Take control of the negative images that you carry around with you. Cut them down to size and imagine them destroyed in any way that takes your fancy: shrivelling away to dust like Dracula, blowing away like desert sand, fading to nothing like a film fading to black. See Section 4 of Chapter 2.

11 Blow it out!

Not quite as rude as it sounds, I hope. Any thought that you find debilitating, whether a memory, a picture or a voice in your head, can be treated with the methods – numbers 7 through 10 – suggested above, and here's a good and positive finale to finish it off and get it well and truly out of your mind. Imagine the once powerful thought as reduced to almost nothing, like a snowflake or ashes. It drops from your mind into your mouth, on to your tongue. Now gently blow it away and out of your head for good. It goes into the atmosphere and is lost. Many people find this kind of visualization helpful, and the accompanying physical act of blowing it away makes it more powerful still.

12 Pray

Lots of people pray and some of them are religious. I'll tread carefully here because, as an agnostic, there may be a view among some readers that I should leave this to those who are signed up to a particular religious belief. I'm not sure that's right, because there's a whole spectrum of belief, from those who 'know' (for example, that there is or isn't something or someone that can be called God), to those who err on one side or the other, to those who struggle with belief or unbelief, to those who really aren't very interested. I find that what I'm most in need of sometimes is the ability to see beyond my own arrogance, and the sense of being part of something bigger is an important aspect of this. Is this prayer? I don't know – it depends on your definition, but here I'm more concerned with the activity and its effectiveness than with what we call it. I also believe that there's great value in using ritual to gain perspective. So setting aside time, for example, to light a candle, quieten your busy mind, compose your thoughts and reflect on the bigger questions of life can be a kind of prayer too – in my understanding anyway!

Prayer, if you can bring yourself to it, is a wonderful way of gaining perspective, whether you pray to a God you believe in, to a 'something that might be there' or to something deep within you. It doesn't have to be tied to a rigid idea of 'belief' – after all, you could write a wonderful and powerful life-changing story without having to believe that it did or ever could actually happen.

If you're embarrassed by the thought, well no one need ever know that you prayed and, if nothing else, it does lift your thoughts to a different plane.

I also know people who find similar value in the rituals of churchgoing yet who don't believe in any of the varieties of Christian doctrine.

13 Write a list and tick something off

Such a simple idea but one that can make a difference because our confidence is often sapped by the thought that we're stuck in a kind of stasis, with seemingly impossible and conflicting demands so keen to get our attention that we feel unable to do anything! One route out of this is simply list what needs to be done and then choose the simplest thing and do it. It might be something as simple as 'buy deodorant' or 'check dog food' or 'change that light bulb'. Go for the simplest thing and do it, and then you have one less thing to worry about. Often people find that the act of listing robs those myriad thoughts of much of their ability to confound and confuse us because we exaggerate things in our mind and once we focus on them by writing them down they become less scary.

You might also find that after a while some things seem to remain on your list when everything else is ticked off; so you can then ask yourself why you don't want to do them. Could it be because they are challenging, or are they things that should never have been on the list in the first place? Perhaps it's something that you want or need to do but recognize that now isn't the right time?

14 Phone a friend

We have these marvellous modern communication technologies available to us: email, text (SMS), instant messaging, internet forums and, of course, phones both fixed-line and mobile. Most of us need never be out of contact with other people, but sometimes there can be a reticence to get in touch, which is often because of a lack of confidence: 'They won't want to speak to me, I'm interfering'; 'I've got nothing to say ...' and so on. Any of these might be true but it's equally likely, perhaps more likely, that your friend is thinking: 'They won't want to speak to me, I'm interfering'; 'I've got nothing to say'! Take the plunge and get in touch, and if you're really worried about not knowing what to say, see the next two tips.

15 Get a phone routine

Some people feel unconfident on the phone, feeling that they don't know what to say, so here are some ideas.

Answering: Work out a routine for answering the phone so that you always have pen and paper nearby and you always ask who is calling and write down their name – if you're trying to remember the name of the person you're talking to you'll be less confident and too distracted by the process.

Put the time of the call down too and, if it's the kind of call where you need to remember things, make notes as you talk – the less you have to retain in your memory, the more you can concentrate on what you and the caller are saying and the more confident you will feel and sound.

Calling: If you're making a call, note down the essential points that you want to get over. This is particularly useful if it's something you feel unconfident about: perhaps an insurance claim or a difficult negotiation with a garage.

Posture: We touched on this in Section 2 of Chapter 2, on body language – just remember that how you stand or sit makes a difference to how you feel and how you sound on the phone.

16 Give yourself the time you need to practise

We often feel foolish about practising things in advance, such as speaking at a meeting or even kicking off a difficult phone call; but why not, if it helps? What you see and hear in your own head isn't how you look and sound to others, so practise out loud in front of a mirror or, better still, with a trusted colleague or friend before any public speaking; and go through your opening before a phone call that you're nervous about, perhaps with some notes. If you're giving a speech or presentation or even introducing a meeting topic, try to practise out loud as this will reveal tricky phrases that look fine on paper but can be difficult to say. This will also reveal any ambiguous-sounding phrases, such as, 'Everyone there was, of course, wearing the bog-standard issue Mao Suit', which could suggest Mickey rather than Mao. See Section 6 of Chapter 2.

17 Go for a walk

Walking is so good for you, on just about every level. Many people, including me, think better, or at least differently, when walking. It puts your energy levels up immediately and it's good for your muscles, heart and digestion. If it's such a miracle, why don't we do more? I guess because it's easier to do nothing, but ultimately, doing nothing drains our energies and thus our confidence. So if you can fit a walk into your daily routine (such as replacing part of your journey to work with a walk), you'll find it worthwhile. You could also add 'take a walk' to your daily list of things to do – one that it's easy to achieve so you get the benefits both of the walk and of being able to tick off something from your list!

18 Get some exercise

Following on from the above, exercise is a great weapon in controlling our moods and helping us not to dwell on our feelings of a lack of confidence. I like swimming as it's good all-round exercise and provides some good thinking time. The thinking time factor is valuable because when you're swimming, rowing, running or whatever, you can't do other things – so you're free to think without distraction (but this doesn't apply when you're road cycling or even running on less safe routes, of course!). Some people like not to think while exercising, preferring instead to go into a more trance-like state to allow the 'processing' to go on in the subconscious.

Any exercise is good for you and, quite apart from the physical benefits and thinking time noted above, the change of pace and activity gingers up your creative abilities, helping you to break out of 'tramline thinking' that can so often be negative and drain confidence.

19 Do something tiny

Is it the big things that worry you and make you feel unconfident? If so, break those big things down into tiny steps. If you're concerned about a job interview, for example, work out small simple steps you can take – really easy stuff like searching the internet for more information on the organization; going to the place where the interview will be so as to practise your route and get the feel of the environment; going through your letter of application with a highlighter to emphasize the key points.

It's so much easier to say, 'I'm going to do this small thing' rather than, 'I've got to prepare really well for this potentially life-changing interview.'

20 Write a letter

Letter-writing is becoming a lost art with so much instant communication available to us, but in truth this isn't solely about letters sent through the post – they can just as easily be delivered by email or in a blog. The important point is to adopt the formality and well-structured approach of the traditional letter. Give yourself time to think through what you want to say, whether it be a letter to a friend, a business letter or a letter of complaint; plan and structure the letter with care so that you convey exactly what you want in the way you want. You can leave it alone and come back to it, even after several days if need be. The confidence factor here is that you give yourself the space you need to do a good, thorough job, rather than dashing something off that you might regret later.

21 Write a journal

Many people find journaling useful. A journal is a daily (usually) personal record of events and thoughts. It can be immensely helpful to recollect the day, gain perspective and understanding about what's happened and record it for looking at again later. In the area of confidence it can help you to keep your feet on the ground by serving as a reminder of what really happened and how you really felt, as opposed to how you've remembered things. You can also use it to track your development over time – you might be surprised that something that seemed so important a month ago is now firmly resolved; or if it's still problematic, this will tell you that you need to focus and work on that area.

22 Talk to your future self

Write a letter to yourself to be opened in a month's or three months' time. Tell yourself what you're feeling and what you hope to have achieved by the time the letter is read. This can be a good way of setting goals and monitoring your progress; it can help you to understand how things change over time, revealing what's really important to you. Don't be too harsh on yourself:

> Dear Gordon,
> I hope by the time you read this you will have finished *The Confidence Book*, be happy with it and have moved on to your next book ...

is better than:

> Dear Gordon,
> I hope and expect that by the time you read this you will have finally pulled your finger out and finished *The Confidence Book...*

23 Make a start

How many projects do you have going on in your head that begin something like, 'One day I'd like to ...'? Choose one and change the opening to, 'Today I'm going to make a start on ...', and commit to getting the ball rolling on that round-the-world trip, that novel, new career or visit to a particular restaurant, spa or whatever fits the bill for you. Age is speaking here, and it's saying that time is always running out; 'One day' will never come unless you make a start.

You may find that making a start in this way leads you on to success, or you may find that once you consider your dream or project in detail, it's not really what you wanted after all – perhaps it was just a vague daydream, for example. There's nothing wrong with daydreams; they can be a great form of escapism. But making a start will tell you what you want to pursue for real and what you'd prefer to keep in the realms of fantasy.

24 Count your positives

If you're reading this then you're literate – one of a tiny percentage of people throughout history who can say this, or write or read it! That's a positive – something encouraging to rejoice in. Focusing on these positives every so often is a good way to feel more energetic and thus more confident.

We used to say 'Count your blessings', and some people feel uneasy about words like 'positives' and 'blessings', preferring to be a little more downbeat and perhaps even cynical. That's our choice, but if we choose to be positive, there is so much to be upbeat about, so much that we take for granted: medical advances, pain-free dentistry, abundant food and, if I dare say it, life itself and the consciousness that gives us a sense of self and the ability to experience the world.

If this is all a bit grand, then focus more narrowly on things that are small-scale, more local, perhaps more recent: that good laugh we shared, the holiday plan we made, that kingfisher we saw today...

We're not going for an unduly rosy view of our life, the universe and everything, just giving a bit of balance when our negative, cynical and confidence-sapping natures take over.

25 Sign up for something

Doing new things can provide a tremendous boost to our confidence and help us to get out of a rut. What could you sign up for? Dancing lessons or a writers' group; a book group or language class? Don't forget charity opportunities, where you can have the benefits of meeting other people and doing some good, all without paying anything out.

The trick is to examine your options and select carefully. If you consider yourself a shy person, go for something where you'll be with other people but not have to speak in front of a whole group – a yoga class might be good here. If you're feeling unconfident about responding to people in conversation, a book group might be a good idea because you can prepare your thoughts in advance and be ready to say, 'I'll have to think about that' if you're put on the spot.

26 Clear your space

'A tidy desk = a tidy mind' – oh yeah! Mess can indicate a creative fusion. I say ignore other people's platitudes and live with the degree of neatness and chaos that works for you – but it can't be a bad thing, every so often, to have a tidy-up and create a fresh working environment. You can chuck away all that stuff that's been sitting around for ages going nowhere, and feel better about yourself in the process; and who knows what you'll find: something you thought long-lost, something you'd completely forgotten, something inspirational?

And the confidence connection? It's one less drag on your positive view of yourself. If it's a mess it's your mess, it's how you want it; and if it's neat and tidy as a freshly pressed shirt, that's your choice too. If your workspace is always neat and tidy, maybe it's time to do something with it!

27 Work on your vision

Do you have an aim, somewhere you want to be, something you want to achieve? A vision is a goal, a big-picture dream. Often we don't openly admit our visions, and sometimes we hide them even from ourselves for fear that we'll look ridiculous if they fail, but a vision is essential. In the book of Proverbs in the Bible, the writer says, 'Where there is no vision the people perish.' I think we can apply this to ourselves as individuals. We need a vision, an aim, a hope against which to measure our actions and to inform the steps we take.

The great thing about a vision of this sort is that in moving towards it, we are achieving it. Supposing you want to write a novel – then go on and admit it. By stating it, even just by writing it down for your eyes only, you'll shape the thought and give it credence – leave it as a vague unspoken idea and it'll never be anything else. Try to be as specific as you can about your vision: is it, for example, a children's novel, an erotic novel, historical fiction? You'll see that by doing the thinking, you're doing the work, and if you write any of it down you really can say, 'I'm writing my novel' without a word of a lie.

Elsewhere in this book I write about the importance of taking small, manageable steps. This is vital, so break your vision down into what you can achieve and set yourself targets.

28 Talk to your past self

Realize how you've changed and how far you've come by holding an imaginary conversation or writing a letter to yourself at a younger age. Try:

Dear Julie,
You've done it. You left your job and five years on you're still here, making a living, doing things you like to do, exploring new opportunities ...

or:

Dear Mahinda,
Don't be upset. You made a mistake, said something you shouldn't have, but it's very much in the past now and you've moved on ...

or:

Dear Jack,
You'll be disappointed to know that you never became an astronaut but, hard as it is for you to accept this, it really doesn't matter now. So much has changed in the 40 years

that separate us, and you feel so differently about lots of things...

29 Create a rule of life

Monastic communities follow a 'rule of life', covering such things as obedience, putting the needs of others first, making time for worship, seeing God in all things and so on. Can you adapt this principle to help you work on your own confidence? Such a rule of life might include:

- I will not measure myself against other people.
- I will examine my core beliefs and seek to adapt them.
- I will not be swayed by negative voices in my head.
- I will find time for reflection and contemplation.
- I will decide my own priorities.

30 Do the ironing

If you're stuck, suffering your own version of 'writer's block' (which I don't believe in, but that's another story), it's better to do something rather than nothing – even that pile of ironing or other chore that you don't fancy. This can jolt you out of negativity and ginger up your thinking, just the undertaking of a physical action in a different place. There's also the distinct possibility that if you're faced with either steaming your way through a pile of ironing or doing something more constructive, you'll opt for something that will enhance your positivity and confidence. You can always make it an aim to earn enough to pay someone else to do your chores – there's an incentive to gain the confidence to achieve!

31 Go somewhere good – physically

Seek out good spaces for a quiet moment or two. Space and silence are important qualities allowing you to gather your thoughts and calm your feelings; they are also prerequisites for many of the activities and processes in this book, so get into the habit of seeking out and noting suitable spaces wherever you are – in and around your workplace, your shopping haunts, on holiday, wherever you find yourself. They could be parks, churches, quiet corners of shopping centres – even the loo will do at a pinch!

There's more on this in Section 1 of Chapter 2, on relaxation.

32 Go somewhere good – mentally

Have an imaginary place, a favourite spot or an invented composite; somewhere you can retreat to for a few minutes' calming relaxation whenever you need it. It only takes a minute or two and can be wonderfully calming and refreshing. Use the relaxation suggestions in this book as your transit system to take you there.

33 Write a short story or a poem

Instead of simply experiencing your lack of confidence, use it as the starting point for a piece of writing. Examine your feelings and thoughts and get them down on paper – either a personal descriptive piece, or put them in the head of an imaginary character. You'll find this therapeutic – it always helps to get our thoughts 'out there'; and also instructive – you'll be thinking about why you think and act as you do. You can also give your story or poem a positive and uplifting end as a way forward is found for your thoughts or the character you've created.

Here are some tips if you're not used to writing this kind of thing:

1 Give yourself two minutes to get started; with the rule that you must keep writing for all that time, even if you just write gibberish or the same words over and over again – just keep writing.

2 Have a break after the initial burst and then go back over what you've written, editing, cutting and revising (easier on a computer for some, but others prefer the tactile quality of pen and paper – there are no hard and fast rules).

3 If it helps you to get started, you can tell yourself that you'll destroy the work as soon as you've read the finished piece – it's for you only and for a limited period of time.

34 Create a work of art

This follows the same principle as the above but applies it to any form of art – clay modelling, drawing or computer graphics, for example. The art is intended for your eyes only and can help you focus on what is blocking your confidence. Here's a simple drawing idea that needs no artistic talent:

1 Draw a line down your page and, on one side, write the word 'Now'. On the other side, write 'Then'. The line represents the confidence factor.

2 On the 'Now' side, create a visualization of how you feel – your lack of confidence; on the 'Then' side represent what you're aiming for. The 'visualization' can be stick-figures, something more developed or something abstract.

3 Draw or write over the line the elements that make up the confidence factor, the things that lead from 'Now' to 'Then'. They could be anything, including ideas in this book, so your line might have: practise, relax, count positives, dress for success – whatever you feel you can do to make 'Then' a reality.

4 Work on the individual ideas you've identified as elements of the line, the 'confidence factor'.

35 Draw your masks

This is another drawing idea. What faces do you show to the world? In other words, what masks do you wear? The able parent, the happy friend, the victim, for example? Be honest with yourself, not about how you feel inside but about how you present yourself in different situations. What effect do your masks have on your confidence? Do you 'fake it to make it' –

that is, act as if you're feeling confident and the confidence itself follows; or do you find that the faking produces an inner lack of confidence that you can't hide? Being aware of our masks can be the first step to inner confidence: we're often not aware of the parts we play and the masks we wear. Maybe you don't have to wear that mask in that situation; maybe you can develop the confidence to be more 'you' and less 'pretend you'.

36 Draw your confidence story as a map

Start with birth and follow a path through various milestones on your road to becoming more or less confident – that is to say, where you think you are now. Some of your map locations may be personal and private, others more public. Does your path appear straight or convoluted? Do you sometimes seem to depart from 'the' path? There are no instructions or rules for how to do this, so give yourself a large blank sheet and simply set out to draw a map of your life in terms of confidence. When you've finished (and you can be as detailed or sketchy as you choose), ask yourself what it tells you about where you've been and where you are now in relation to confidence issues. Can you project your map a month, a year or five years into the future?

37 See life on a screen

Borrow this technique from Buddhist philosophy: step back and try to see life as 'out there', as if projected on a screen. You watch and observe but remain detached, without being caught up in emotional turmoil. You won't want to live like this all the time but it can help you gain perspective and see things differently in short bursts.

38 Throw a die

You need a die, paper and a pen. Write down six things you want to do that require confidence (follow the advice throughout this book to make your ideas achievable and clear). Number your list and decide that, today, as soon as possible, you are going to do one of those things. Throw the die, look up the number – and do it!

39 Sing

Many people swear by singing as a classic (or pop!) way of getting out of yourself, of being active and physical, of rejoicing in your abilities. Will this work for you? You can sing on your own but you'll get a lot more confidence (and not just in singing – it's transferable) if you sing with others in a group or choir or at church, for example; after all, many people go to church who can't sign up to the full set of beliefs, but like the community aspects, the music and the chance to think.

40 Play random word association

This is a powerful and fun way of getting your creative juices flowing and helping you to feel more confident if you're stuck in your thinking. Use a dictionary: open it at random and point to any word without looking. Now create a connection between the problem you're working on and the word you've just found. It's often easier than you think. I've just done it and come up with the word 'direct' – so I could say that this exercise is a clear and direct way of gingering up your thinking; or I could use it to ask myself if I'm being too directive in my approach as I write this section. The confidence factor here is that so often we get stuck with the same thoughts and ideas; this exercise can jolt us out of this and turn our attention in new directions. See also Section 8 of Chapter 2.

41 Look up

The theory is that you can't connect with your negative feelings if you lift your eyes and your head heavenward. So simple but so true? Well, maybe! Give it a go when you're feeling unconfident and make it part of your routine just before situations where you need to be at your best, such as meetings, job interviews or occasions where you often feel your confidence undermined. See more in Section 5 of Chapter 2.

42 Do that thing you used to do

What is there that you used to do with confidence – ice skating, writing letters, pottery? Why did you stop and could you get something out of restarting?

43 Work out your prompts

Giving a speech or speaking at a meeting or event? Find a way to give yourself the support you need, such as notes, cue cards, key words. Find your own system that works best for you, giving you the support you need. Once you have them you won't need them as much as if you didn't have them! See more in Section 6 of Chapter 2.

44 Map your feelings

Ask yourself where your confidence-sapping feelings seem to be located in your body. Then massage them away either physically or with the power of imagination. It sounds bizarre but once you start to think about your feelings you'll realize that they all seem rooted in some part of your body. Having a physical location to think about can help you to concentrate on imagining the feelings being gently eased away or even expelled from your body. See more in Section 5 of Chapter 2.

45 Be prepared

If you find certain social or formal situations awkward, do your homework in advance. Find out about who will be there, or the building, the area or some peripheral information about the issue you're there to discuss. You're looking for anything that will give you a conversation starter to fill those awkward moments. There's more in Section 7 of Chapter 2.

46 Take the focus off yourself

An extension of the above is to take something with you that can take the focus away from you, perhaps something related to the venue or the subject of the event – an article, postcard or photograph, for example. See also Section 7 of Chapter 2.

47 Laugh

Annette Goodheart is one of the best-known 'laughter coaches'. She believes in the power of laughter to boost our immune system, get us out of our emotional ruts and, among other things, bring us closer to others. She believes that we don't laugh because we're happy; we're happy because we laugh. You can find out more at her website and those of other laughter therapists – see <www.teehee.com>.

Many who work in this field believe that we don't need something funny to get us laughing; we can just start to laugh and the laughter then takes over. Whatever you think about this particular approach, there can be no doubt that 'laughter is a tonic'. It relaxes us, helps us to gain perspective and, in terms of confidence, can break us away from negative thoughts and feelings. So give it a go and add a good laugh to your confidence-boosting strategies!

48 Carry your own loyalty card

Write down a list of positive beliefs to carry around with you, perhaps on a credit-card-sized card; three is a good number. For example:

- I believe that I know what I'm talking about in my job.
- I believe that others have different skills from me and I don't have to compete on every level.
- I believe that my quieter, more focused approach is valuable in the workplace and that others agree with me.

See another example and how to arrive at this point in Section 4 of Chapter 2.

49 Take time to reflect

Understanding a thing helps to rob it of its power to hurt us, so when you've been in a situation that saps your confidence, give it time to settle in your mind so that you're not so emotionally caught up in it. And then reflect on it. You're trying to understand why you were affected in this way. Does it relate to core beliefs (see Section 4 of Chapter 2)? Does it remind you of other events? How much was it related to other factors, such as recent events, your mood and so on? Was there a mixture of factors and can you unpick and begin to understand them? You might find it useful to keep a brief journal so that over time you can look back and understand things in context.

50 Take a break

If you walk away from something and forget about it for a while, you understand it better when you come back to it. This is true of crosswords and, I'm told, number puzzles like Su Doku. It is certainly true, in my experience, of learning lines, writing, and all manner of creative endeavours. So don't be afraid to leave things alone for a bit. It's not necessarily an unwillingness to get on with things, or laziness (though sometimes it is for me!); and it can give your subconscious time to process the issue. Leave it long enough and the way forward might pop up in a dream, in conversation or when idly daydreaming. See more in Section 8 of Chapter 2.

51 Feelings, thoughts and core beliefs

Try to understand the relationship between these. Your feelings grow out of your thoughts and these are influenced by core beliefs that you have about yourself. So if you find yourself feeling nervous about meeting a particular person, try to track back to the thought that preceded and ignited the feeling. It might be, 'She'll make me look a fool.' The core belief behind this would be, 'Other people are better than me; they show me up.' Understanding is one part of the solution; working on your core beliefs is another. See more in Section 4 of Chapter 2.

52 Toss a coin but not for a chance result

Can't make up your mind and feel a lack of confidence because of it? Use the trick of picking two options and tossing a coin. Note how you feel when, for example, heads come up for 'Go on that date' – pleased? Then go. Still not convinced? Shelve the idea or do some more thinking about it. The tossing of the coin isn't about letting luck decide for you; it's about noting your reactions and using these as a guide. See another example in Section 3 of Chapter 2.

53 Think about what you wear

Some of you will devote considerable time to choosing your clothes for any occasion, but as a different way of looking at it, take three items of clothing you have worn recently and ask yourself in each case: What functions does this have? Try to get a handle on why you wear what you do. Is it comfort, sexiness, power dressing, to make you stand out or to help you blend in? Use this knowledge to help you dress for confidence in each situation. See more about clothes in Section 3 of Chapter 2.

54 This is the face that...

Are you self-conscious about your face, comparing your looks to societal norms and ideals? Think about your face in a different way, as a mirror of your life, and draw confidence from all that you have lived through your face. It's much more than a fashion statement could ever be: this is the face that took my first breath, tasted home cooking, I offered to my lover ... You can find out more about this exercise in Section 3 of Chapter 2.

55 Exercise your face

Before you go into a situation where you have to speak, give your face a workout – probably in the loo, where your facial gymnastics won't be interrupted. Or if you want to try tongue-twisters you'll perhaps be better off in an open space away from other people – unless you simply want to be confident about it and let others 'deal' if they have a problem with your exercising your face! Imagine chewing an ever growing piece of gum that gives your mouth and lips a real workout as it gets bigger and bigger and as your jaws stretch to accommodate it and your tongue gyrates around your mouth! You'll speak better for giving your speaking apparatus a warm-up, just as you'd warm up your body before dancing or running. This kind of exercise can also distract you from your concerns about the event itself, giving you a practical focus – something to do as you wait to 'go on'. There's more, including tongue-twisters, in Section 3 of Chapter 2.

56 Doublethink

Thinking can often be a sort of dialogue in which we tell ourselves one thing but are aware of another thought behind it and another behind that. No? Must just be me then! If we have them, those subconscious and semi-conscious thoughts can betray us, as in the famous Freudian slip (parapraxia):

- You know what a Freudian slip is, right?
- No.
- Well, it's when you think one thing and say your mother.

It's self-evident that we can't be aware of our subconscious thoughts, but we can be aware of self-censorship – you have an idea, but attached to it at the hip is the thought, 'I can't say that. People will laugh' or 'I can't say that. It's too obvious' or 'It'll be rejected out of hand by X and X.' The doublethink may be helpful in the right situation, but it's important to be aware of it and choose whether to follow it or not; otherwise it just saps confidence and we don't stop to think why.

I had a quick bit of doublethink when writing the above: Should I use 'attached to it at the hip'? Is it right to use a debilitating medical condition in this way when many other options are available to me? And then the double-doublethink that I could use this very question as a further example of doublethink! There's a further example in Section 3 of Chapter 2.

57 Look into my eyes (almost)

Find it difficult to look someone in the eye? Look at their eyebrows instead – they won't know the difference and you'll find it less awkward. See more about eye contact in Section 2 of Chapter 2.

58 Do a workshop

Even I can't claim that this fabulous book is all you need, and since I hope you've bought it already, I can admit that you can also learn a great deal from workshops and seminars, having a go at confidence-building in a supportive environment. There are many workshops available, ranging from dreamwork to presentation skills, and from body language to meditation. The web addresses of some of those offering this sort of thing are in the Acknowledgements.

59 Zone in on your hands

Explore Mark Bowden's ideas (introduced in Section 2 of Chapter 2) about the different planes your hands can move in. Practise using your hands to gesture below the waist (the Grotesque-Plane), at the belly button (Truth-Plane) and at chest height (the Passion-Plane). What effect does this have on your effectiveness and thus your confidence?

60 Changing your stance

Train yourself to become more aware of your body language. Do you tend to use distracting mannerisms, such as rocking back and forth as you speak? Does your hand drift in front of your face, sending unconscious negative signals? Practise some comfortable stances that look and feel natural to you, and make these part of your repertoire, particularly in formal situations such as running a meeting or giving a presentation. If you can arrange a video of yourself in action this can be powerfully revealing. Do allow yourself to get over the 'Don't I look awful' stage that many people experience when they see themselves on video, and move on quickly to the realization that a few simple changes to posture and use of space can make a big difference to your effectiveness. There are lots more tips in Section 2 of Chapter 2.

61 Picture and wordplay

If you've got something tricky to learn, use pictograms, acronyms and wordplay to help you remember it. Suppose you had to learn: 'I'd like to introduce the chair of our society, a former president of the French Institute for Foreign Affairs and, perhaps more relevant to us, currently promoting chocolate éclairs and a regular contributor to *Marie Claire*. Please welcome...'

You can remember all the bits, but not necessarily in the right order – is she President of Marie Claire or a contributor to *Foreign Affairs*?

As you're learning your bit, you could use the fact that you're introducing a French woman to help you think of the acronym FEM, which helps you get the order right – Foreign, Éclairs, *Marie Claire*; or you could get a picture in your mind of a map of France that you lift to reveal a picture of an éclair that you then see is in a copy of *Marie Claire*. There are lots of ways to help you remember tricky stuff, and more are explored in Section 6 of Chapter 2.

62 Take notes

If you find yourself in a difficult work relationship, take notes of any incidents that you think show inappropriate comments or behaviour. When you reread them, they'll help you gain perspective – perhaps in hindsight you can see that you overreacted; on the other hand, if over time you see a pattern emerging, you'll have a useful account to help your case should it go to tribunal or management review.

63 1 + 1 = New

Use your creative side to put ideas together. We're all creative; it's part of the human condition, part of how we learn and think. Believing yourself to be 'not a creative person' is one of the more confidence-sapping ideas we can have, so give your creativity a workout using the ideas explored in the Quintessence method in Section 8 of Chapter 2.

Conclusion

Well, that's it. I do hope that this has given you a few ideas to be going on with. When I say a few, what I really mean is one idea at a time. Take it little by little. This is the most simple, practical way to kick off your confidence, and fits in well with the nature of this book.

Think of just one thing related to confidence that you want to make progress on. It could be a phone call you need to make but are nervous about, or something you want to say to someone that needs courage; it could be about being prepared to speak at a meeting or to ask for a pay rise; anything that you'd like to do but feel unable to because of a lack of confidence.

Having chosen your 'issue', don't dwell on what you feel, but do consider being as accurate and clear as possible about what you want to do. Avoid woolly generalizations: not 'I'd like to say a bit more at meetings' but 'At tomorrow's meeting I'm going to say something about the air conditioning.'

Having been clear, be kind: don't set yourself an impossible task and don't see the outcome as a Hollywood-style climax with surging music, growing applause and a triumph for our previously silent hero. Instead, ask yourself what small step you can take to make progress, and work out how you can do it. You're not going to get the air conditioning sorted tomorrow, but you could raise the issue and ask for comments. Write out a couple of clear sentences and have them with you to refer to, such as: 'I'm concerned that the air conditioning doesn't seem to be working very well in our corner of the office. I wonder how others in our section feel – do you agree?' This is something you can achieve; you can plan for it, give yourself support and make real progress.

In this instance you could also show your question to one or two people in advance to see if they will support you.

An important aspect of this is to think about what will happen afterwards, as well as the action you will take in the meeting. Keep your focus clearly on your goal, which is to raise the issue, but don't allow yourself to become despondent if, having raised it, nothing seems to happen immediately. In fact, this is what you should expect. It is so important that you don't allow your budding confidence to be squashed because you don't seem to make much progress. Allow yourself time to reflect on and emphasize what you have achieved. Even if you were unable to say your piece because of lack of time or because others hogged the meeting, you've done the preparation and that's a real step forward – and there'll be another chance to use it at the next meeting.

Step by step and a little at a time: these are the ways to build confidence – and, of course, you might come out of that first meeting with real progress.

For many readers this will seem like a small thing, but I've met plenty of people who would find this challenging – the key is to be clear, make an achievable plan, and give yourself support. This book offers lots of ways to achieve this, and if you do need more support, there are plenty of organizations and groups that can help. Do have a look at those I've listed in the Acknowledgements at the beginning of this book, and don't forget The Confidence Site <www.theconfidencesite.co.uk>, where you'll find more tips and ideas and can post your own thoughts – and good luck!

Index